To Comfort
All Who Mourn

The spirit of the Lord GOD is upon me,
  because the LORD has anointed me;
He has sent me to bring glad tidings to the lowly,
  to heal the brokenhearted,
To proclaim liberty to the captives
  and release to the prisoners,
To announce a year of favor from the LORD
  and a day of vindication by our God,
  to comfort all who mourn.... (Isaiah 61:1-2)

To Comfort All Who Mourn

*A Parish Handbook
For Ministry to the Grieving*

Carol Luebering

This is a revised edition of the book
originally published by Celebration Books.

Cover design by Julie Lonneman.
Cover illustration by Joseph Roy.
SBN 0-86716-045-4

Contents

Introduction

In the city where I live, a woman lost a son suddenly and tragically. She and her husband had long been active in their parish, and the whole community rallied in support when the child died.

One day, a few months after the boy's funeral, her phone rang. A quiet woman she had met once or twice at PTA meetings poured out her agony. She too had lost a son and her grief was unbearable. How, she asked, could a mother continue to face life after experiencing such a loss?

The first woman admitted to sleepless nights and haunting memories, to days when pain seemed certain to overwhelm her. But she also spoke of the support of friends, the people who filled the church to overflowing for the funeral, who brought casseroles and listened to her memories, who reached for her hand whenever her son's favorite song was played at morning mass. "I suppose that's what keeps me going," she answered.

"But I have had none of that," said the flat voice on the phone, and the line went dead.

That phone call might have been made in any parish, in yours or—until recently—in mine.

A few years ago in my parish, a group of caring people came together to form a ministry team in service to the bereaved. Our commitment is to assure that no member of our community grieves alone, without the love, the practical skills, the resurrection faith we hold in trust for one another.

Those of us who serve in this ministry have found these years a time of rapid learning and many surprises. For our parish, it has been a period of unparalleled growth in love. For me personally, ministering to grieving people has been the most rewarding experience in a life overflowing with gifts. My small world has been widened by cherished friends I would otherwise not have known— friends who have been generous enough to share their deepest pain, their most fearsome inadequacies with me. Most of all, I have discovered how little room the Lord needs to move freely. Incredibly, even I can make his presence tangible.

An apology

I am a Roman Catholic, baptized as an infant into that tradition. My church is certainly not without defect; I bear a share of the scars its people inflict on one another. But it has the feel of home. Love for this flawed institution holds me in spite of the questions that surface from time to time.

Yet I came to faith in an ecumenical setting. The social concern and sense of community held by my Protestant friends helped bring to life all I had learned about Jesus Christ. To them I acknowledge a debt I can never repay.

My words are framed by the Catholic experience. It is the only language I can speak. But I hope they strike an echo in hearts bound to other traditions and contribute to the vision we share in Jesus Christ, risen and present with us all.

I hope this book will help you to minister to the grieving in your midst. I can share with you the fruits of our experience and suggest some possibilities we have not yet explored. But in the end the gifts your community can bring to the task are a wealth only you can explore fully.

So I pray you may find the courage (and it does take courage!) to share the weight of the crosses that bow other shoulders and find walking beside you the wounded but triumphant man from Nazareth.

Part One

Exploring
the Possibilities

1

A People Sent to Comfort

Christians are people who proclaim in their creed and in their lives Jesus Christ's death and resurrection. In him, we profess that death, the human race's ultimate enemy, has been forever overcome. Though death still walks among us, stealing friend and spouse, child and parent, we have no faith in its power. In the risen Jesus we are one; any separation is temporary and illusory.

As Christians, we pray for our dead, commending them into divine hands which will reunite us. In every celebration of the eucharist, we remember those who have gone before us. And a mass card is still the first gift Catholics think to offer sorrowing families.

As Christians, we care for the living. Our faith asserts that when the kingdom now unfolding comes to full flower, every tear will be wiped away; and love, creation's greatest and most enduring element, will know no disappointment. To those who sorrow at the death of a loved one, we speak a hope that transcends everything the human race has ever dreamed.

Still, we wander far from our kingdom home. In a wounded world, we must cling to one another for the assurance that the hope we hold is not mere hallucination. In the love we receive from one another—the love that marks and identifies us as Christians—we discover in our lives the truth that love formed and rules the universe.

At least, some of us do. When tragedy strikes people deeply involved in our community, we are aware of their pain and quick to extend our sympathy and support. Furthermore, the actively involved are accustomed to look to the church in their need. They are perhaps readier than most to acknowledge their helplessness, their dependence on the gifts our Father pours out in foolish, unlimited bounty.

But not all of us have acquired the habit of mutual dependence. Even in the smallest parish, there are those whose participation is minimal, who live almost as strangers among us. When death touches them, they turn in need to the church for perhaps the first time, seeking the rites of burial.

A communal failure

Too often, a funeral service is all they get. If meals are provided for the mourners, if a sympathetic ear is available to help them sort out their feelings in the months after the funeral, if kind hands help with the practical problems death creates, it is by accident, not as a conscious gesture of a caring faith community.

Even the rites may be shorn of their rich possibilities. Without prior experience in worship planning, most people are reluctant to take any responsibility for the liturgy. A celebrant who chooses the readings and plans a homily without knowing either the dead or the survivors can only preach abstractions. He may or may not touch the faith questions in the pews before him. The organist's favorite hymns may offer no comfort; they may not even be familiar. The caring presence of the community's liturgical ministers—lectors, cantors, communion ministers—is likely to be missing.

The purpose of the revised funeral rite, according to its introduction, is not only to commend the dead into God's hands but also to console the living and nurture their faith. Like all the church's rituals, it is a *communal* celebration, drawing on the community's faith and gifts to make the Lord's presence tangible. And like any of the church's rituals, it rings hollow if the love and faith expressed in the rite find no echo in believers' lives. Offering consolation and nurturing one another's faith must be a continuing task—or it is a failed task.

The death of a loved one shakes a person's world to its foundation. In the face of the unspeakable mystery of human mortality, everything held in faith acquires a new meaning; urgent questions arise. Grieving people cry out for meaning, for security, for belief in a compassionate God who brings life out of death.

We believe in resurrection. We hold the hope mourners long to feel. If we speak of eternal life only for their dead, we have not said enough. Something dies in a survivor, too. Part of the self is laid in a loved one's grave; what remains must be brought again to life.

Death takes more than a person with whom we shared thoughts and joys and sorrows. It steals our sense of identity as once defined by the relationship. A woman without a husband is no longer wife but widow. A man who buries his firstborn is robbed of his proud and tender sense of fatherhood. Even though he has other children, he has failed to protect this child from harm.

The search for a new identity, the struggle to accept oneself as a whole person in a strange new role is the work of grieving. Successfully completed, it leads to a kind of resurrection, the rising of a new and independent life from the ruins of the old. To the extent that anyone among us undertakes that struggle alone and grieves in painful isolation, we the Christian community have failed in our call to bear witness to the risen Lord's power.

A community called to heal

It's easy to lay the blame at the rectory door. Certainly some fault is there; many a tale of alienation begins with a pastor's failure to minister adequately to a stricken family. Ordained clergy are wholly human. They can be too busy, preoccupied, thoughtless or careless.

But the best, most giving among them are subject to the same limitations that beset the rest of us. They can be in just one place at a time, and the grace of ordination has never added an hour to anyone's day.

In any case, the community is not to be equated with its pastoral staff. We are all of us together the Spirit-gifted body of Christ. All of us are transient. We may move after two years or die after 50. Our pastoral staff is definitely transient. Called to serve for five years or 10, they will leave us. The community life goes on.

Like any living entity, the community has a unique personality. If my parish or yours is experienced as warm and loving, it is because you and I and a lot of other people give of ourselves to create the climate. Because so many of us radiate the Lord's healing presence, the wounded find a home with us.

In first-century Palestine, the wounded always came to Jesus. The sick and the lame, the blind, the sinful and the rejected found their way to him and asked for healing. And he responded.

It is no different today. Those in the most desperate need are most open to Christ's touch; the self-sufficient have never sought him. The death of someone significant leaves a wound slow to heal, subject to infection: spiritual agony and festering questions, crippling practical needs and aching loneliness. Those who grieve know they are not self-sufficient. They are ready to come to the Lord for healing. If they feel his touch, really feel it, they respond with deepened faith. Where will they find him if not in us?

We acknowledge we are Christ's body, his presence on earth. But when we try to exercise his healing power we are brought up against our own limitations. Jesus of Nazareth held power over death. He restored Jairus' daughter to her parents' arms, gave a son back to the widow of Naim and called Lazarus out of his tomb. That power has not been given to us. In all the Spirit-gifted community there is no one who can warm death's chill or erase the pain it inflicts. We are helpless.

In the hope we hold in Jesus Christ, we can affirm that loss is not real or permanent. But confronted with another person's tears and sorrow our words may sound hollow even to our ears. Knowing we cannot work miracles, we lose sight of the gifts we can bring and we do nothing.

But Jesus' ministry was not limited to miraculous intervention. The gospels are filled with his concern for ordinary, everyday needs. He noted that Jairus' daughter was hungry, that Lazarus was bound by his grave wrappings. He addressed himself to the simple needs for food and freedom of movement even as he exercised his power over death.

His people can do the same. They can make hundreds of simple gestures to support the sorrowing—gestures that can help turn them toward the future. Together we have an abundance of gifts to offer in healing.

2

Real Needs, Real Ministry

Human needs are complex and interwoven. In infancy, the need
for food and the need for warm physical contact find expression in
the same cry. As adults, we find it difficult to pinpoint the primary
lack that throbs at the center of our lives.

Grieving people find it even more difficult to speak their needs
clearly. It is inadequate to say they have pain. They simply *are* an
empty ache. Well-meaning friends, speaking from their uncertainty,
are quick to ask if there is anything they can do, but the response is
usually negative. Nothing, it seems, could really help.

But any caring gesture can speak comfort, just as a cool hand on a
child's feverish forehead soothes the hurt in body and spirit. The
friend who calls with a casserole, with plans for an outing or with a
simple expression of concern does not fill the emptiness of loss. But
the warmth of the gesture surrounds the emptiness with healing
tenderness.

The first step, then, in organizing a parish ministry to the
bereaved is to decide what gestures the community can offer and to
enlist people whose time and talents fit the task.

The gestures are limited only by our imaginations. In general,
there are three areas of ministry: *liturgical, practical* and *supportive*.
Frequently they overlap, but each has particular requirements.

Liturgical ministry

Liturgical ministry is the *most obvious* effort we can make to comfort
the bereaved. Worship is the activity which most truly forms and
expresses our identity as a Christian community. And the need to

bury the dead with prayer and ritual is one for which everyone looks first to the church—even those whose lives are seldom touched by churchly concerns. Burying the dead is a gesture we already offer; but we can do much to enrich it.

The revised funeral rite gives Catholic families options they never before had to consider: choice of words, songs and gestures to reflect their precious memories and personal faith.

Some Catholics are sufficiently well-versed in liturgy planning to undertake the task unaided. Many more do not understand what is involved, much less where to begin. Few priests can afford to give much time to assist; most can only offer the family an opportunity to look over the readings. The burden often falls on funeral directors, who may be willing and capable, but they also suffer time limitations as well as uncertainty about policies that differ from parish to parish.

Trained volunteers can give time to grieving families, if the group is large enough to spread the responsibilities. People who help plan a funeral liturgy occasionally can give a great deal of time to each one. It is no burden to spend several hours exploring the possibilities with a family if the occasion arises once in two or three months.

The principles and procedures we follow in my parish are outlined below (see pages 37-44). We find that the appreciation families express is ample reward for the time we invest, and this care is quickly apparent to the community at large. A bereavement ministry does not exist to call attention to itself, but it does contribute much to a parish's growing sense of itself as a loving, serving people.

The people who serve the community in its Sunday worship are a real gift to the bereaved. Good lectors bring to life the readings a family selects and release the healing power of God's word. Funeral congregations are extraordinarily attentive to the readings. They hunger to believe that this death, however senseless it may seem, is rich with promise. They are, in a very real sense, a gift returned to lectors. They affirm the importance of the ministry.

Communion ministers can offer the cup as well as assist in the distribution of the bread. Long periods of silence are difficult at a funeral: unwelcome thoughts crowd the mind and block the heart's prayer. Even more than at the Sunday liturgy, the distribution of communion at a funeral mass should not be excessively long.

Musical support is crucial at a funeral. It is hard to sing with a lump in the throat—and the more appropriate the songs, the larger the lump seems. A cantor or volunteer choir—composed of homemakers or retired people—can carry the burden of song and give cracking voices something to lean on. They can do songs that are comforting but unfamiliar to the congregation.

The list of liturgical ministries goes on and on—ushers to welcome people and seat them near the family, volunteer pallbearers when needed, typists to prepare a program booklet, skilled writers to craft a prayer of the faithful to the family's needs.

But the most important ministry a community offers at a funeral is the presence of its people. There are funerals that fill the church. There are others for the person who has outlived family and friends, languishing alone in a nursing home until death. A funeral attended by only a handful of mourners is a sad and lonely affair. The presence even of strangers, ministering from the sanctuary or from the pews, affirms the community's conviction that every one of its members, living or dead, is precious and irreplaceable.

The funeral mass is not our only opportunity to minister to the liturgical needs of bereaved families. Shared prayer at the funeral home is a Catholic tradition, whether it be the familiar rosary or the scripture service outlined in the funeral rite. Prayer at the graveside is painful farewell spoken in the Lord's presence. When no priest is available on either occasion, a member of the ministry team can lead people in prayer.

During the year, a carefully planned memorial mass offers survivors the promise that their dead are not forgotten and that we still know and pray for the needs of the living. The feast of All Souls (November 2), the Easter season, even some of the Sundays of the year could be occasions for this remembrance. A personal invitation to everyone who has suffered a recent loss, either by mail or in person from people in close contact, speaks warm and tender care. A reception after mass underscores our personal concern and brings the grieving into contact with one another. They have in common what is important to all of us: they are united by Christ's cross in a way the rest of us can only try to understand.

Prayer with and for the sorrowing is constant in our ministry. It begins when the news of death spreads through the group; a round robin of phone calls or a single volunteer on the phone provides the cue. It continues as one person quietly prays with another who is in pain, or the ministry group itself gathers to pray. No one grieves alone when surrounded by the prayers of other believers.

Ministry to practical needs

Practical assistance is the *easiest* ministry we can offer. It draws on people's everyday skills: cooking, driving, babysitting, simple household repairs. The talents are there in the community, waiting to be called into service.

At the time of death, a family is overwhelmed by details that need attention. Notifying relatives and friends, choosing caskets and cemetery plots, receiving condolences—all occupy an amazing amount of time. There may also be special needs such as meeting out-of-town relatives at the airport or finding a sitter for an infant grandchild while the family is at church. A bereaved family has little time or energy for meeting mundane needs—feeding people or keeping them supplied with clean underwear.

Traditionally, neighbors busied themselves with those needs. But in our increasingly urban and mobile society, neighbors are not always the reliable source they once were. Part of our task may be to alert neighbors to the death and to help organize their support. Where neighborhood resources are lacking or inadequate, we as Christians are called to be neighbor.

The time between death and burial is not only a period of acute need, but also the moment when people are willing to accept what is offered. Even when death has been expected, it still comes as a surprise. For perhaps the first time in their lives, people discover their dependence on others' care. Any help that appears at the door is gratefully received as a gift of love.

Food is the first need. Farflung families suddenly find themselves under one roof. The press of urgent decisions may drive the thought of eating out of mind, but appetites usually reassert themselves when food appears on the table. Teenagers, of course, are a fantastic drain on the refrigerator's contents. (As the mother of a 16-year-old boy, I can testify that no calamity can faze the adolescent appetite!)

On the day of the funeral, the need grows. In the rush to get to church on time, there may be no chance to prepare a hearty breakfast. Because a long morning stretches ahead, coffeecakes and rolls are a generous blessing.

After the funeral, families gather once more, usually over lunch. Even at day's end, when relatives and friends have left, a meal will again be appreciated. (When my mother-in-law lay dying, kind friends fixed our meals while we spent the last week of her life at the hospital; they provided a banquet after the funeral. That evening, I was astonished to discover we had nothing in the house for dinner.)

Child care is another need at the time of death. Energetic toddlers underfoot, however wearing, are in some way a comfort—an assurance that life does indeed go on. But sometimes there is a need for quiet. Solemn conversation at the funeral home or prayer in church can be an ordeal both for very small children and for the adults who must try to keep them under control. A volunteer babysitter for tiny tots gives other family members a chance to deal with their grief.

Tiny tots, that is. Naturally enough, we want to protect our children from all unpleasantness. But the mind of a child old enough to realize that something unusual is going on (and that would certainly include most three-year-olds and some children even younger) is already shaping some concept of death. Exposure to the reality and honest answers to questions draws a picture much less terrifying than a child's active imagination creates. We encourage parents to take children to the funeral home for a little while, even to the funeral services if they wish. When they (or their guardian elders) have had enough, then we whisk them off to play.

Children are not the only people who need "babysitters." An invalid, a senile grandparent, a profoundly retarded adult may be excluded by circumstances from the funeral rites, but not from the community. We can keep them company, even join with them in prayer. And if someone brings communion from the funeral mass, the link with the communal worship will be complete.

If relatives are coming from out of town and must be met at public terminals, the family's automotive resources can be severely strained, especially with appointments to keep at the funeral home and the cemetery. Making cars and drivers available to meet travelers or run simple errands relieves the strain.

Some deaths must be made known in a lot of circles. Breaking the news to the closest people belongs to the family, but we can help contact more distant friends and coworkers.

In many urban areas, the newspaper obituary column serves as a kind of classified advertising for burglars. A person to stay in the house during visitation and funeral services not only insures against unwelcome intrusion, but relieves the bereaved of this anxiety.

When the funeral is over and life begins to settle into a strangely unfamiliar routine, practical needs continue to arise. They are as varied as the circumstances of the bereaved. The removal of an adult from a family circle means that his or her responsibilities must be assumed by someone else—for whom they may be totally unfamiliar. A helping hand or two eases the transition.

Sometimes the needs are obvious. A widower with children may need help in learning to manage the kitchen and the laundry—not to mention shopping for a daughter's first bra. The death of a husband who always assumed the car and house maintenance as his special province may leave a widow foundering helplessly in the hands of unscrupulous repairmen. Finding a way through the maze of social security questions is a chore for which most dependents appreciate a guiding hand.

Other needs are less obvious but no less real. A widow living alone may manage meals efficiently but never want to bake a cake she has to eat alone. Sharing a dessert consoles the sweet tooth while lifting loneliness. Carrying the double load of financial support and the care of house and children is a burden for the surviving adult. A casual dinner invitation would be a loving gesture.

Because practical needs are diverse in the months after a funeral, they are more difficult to serve than needs at the time of death. The community's care depends on discernment of need. While friends and relatives may be sensitive enough to notice the need and sufficiently acquainted with the community's resources to draw on them, the primary responsibility for making help available falls on the ministry team. Effective care depends on contact with bereaved people throughout the period of mourning.

Long-term support

This contact with grieving people in the months after death is the least obvious need we are called to serve; but it is the *most important*. No other gift means so much to the sorrowing. Long-term support is the most critical element in a successful program of ministry to the bereaved.

In recent years psychologists have turned their attention to grief. They have found that loss is not a single, simple event. Grief is not just what one feels at a death. Rather, it is a *process* to be worked through in a welter of confusing, sometimes conflicting emotions.

An understanding of what bereaved people suffer is an essential skill for people who want to minister to the sorrowing. I will discuss grief more fully later (see pages 63-67); but, for now, I want to emphasize the two most characteristic marks of grief since they affect the planning of a ministry program.

Grief is a long process

Life quickly returns to a semblance of normality in the weeks after the funeral. Even those most deeply stricken return to work, assume household management and begin to plan for the future. On the outside, they seem to be making a fine adjustment.

But inside, the loss is raw and new. Or rather, the loss is not inside at all, but an external event that has taken control of life's details. It takes a long time to internalize death's reality—even to believe it is real—and to integrate the changes it brings to a survivor's life. Hardly anyone achieves full integration in less than a year. For many people, it takes two or three years.

The structure of a year is a factor that prolongs grief. We are creatures who live in time. We mark the days and weeks, the months and seasons. We count the dates with special significance—holidays, birthdays, anniversaries—dates inextricably associated with the people we love.

Remove someone central from a life and the meaning of those dates shifts painfully. Now there is a Christmas with no reason to buy toys for a dead child, a birthday for which no wife will bake a cake. There is a spring the garden lies untouched by hands that loved the soil, the fall a husband does not put up the storm windows. Every day, every season whose meaning was shaped by the dead person is a time when loss is a fresh stab of pain, when the realization of death's permanence comes home a little harder.

Death crowds the family calendar with new and bleak anniversaries: a month ago he died, three months since her last trip to the hospital, the anniversary of the day the fatal illness was diagnosed, the month we bought the car in which he died. Even weekdays assume a new significance. If Tuesday was the day of death, Tuesday after Tuesday stands as a stark reminder.

The nature of the grief process also prolongs mourning. A certain numbness, a kind of merciful anesthesia cushions the initial blow. It wears off slowly over weeks or months. We learn by degrees that separation is for the rest of a lifetime. Important dates slip by before that realization dawns fully; the second Christmas may well be the one that feels most empty.

In time, all the anniversaries are marked with pain; in enough time, all the anniversaries are rediscovered as something one can survive. The most significant—the day of death, the wedding anniversary—may draw tears for years to come. But for the most part, the loss is reduced to a manageable size, an ache noticed by a newly whole person.

Ultimately, time alone has little power to heal the wounds left by death. Grief is a process to be *worked* through. Time helps, but time does not do the work. The grieving persons do. They face the task of internalizing the awful reality, accepting the loss and developing a sense of self no longer defined by an interrupted relationship.

There is something that heals. We hold it. As Christians, we live in time but we are not shackled by it. We also live in a world beyond time, the kingdom unfolding in our midst. We have touched the eternal reality and found its face is love. Love heals in and beyond time. No one knows that better than we do, because we have been touched by Christ's love and brought to new and lasting life.

Grief is a lonely process

The loss of a love—even when that love was fraught with difficulty and disagreement—precipitates pain. Every loss is as unique as the relationship disrupted. And every relationship is as unique as the two persons involved. No one ever suffers the same loss as another, even though they grieve for the same person. No one can really understand; no one can feel the exact throb of another's pain. Loneliness is an essential part of grief.

The loneliness is compounded by others' expectations. A widow who weeps at her husband's funeral receives her friends' sympathy. But if her tears are still falling six months later—as well they might —the same friends are likely to say it is time she pulled herself together.

For all she knows, they are right. After all, the role is new to her; a widow's grief is as unfamiliar to her as to her still-wed friends. The models held up for her emulation have always been the stoic, the courageous, the undefeated. In sorrowing over her husband's death, she begins to feel she is a failure as a human being. She is faced with a choice between causing isolation from others by revealing the pain she feels or causing isolation from herself by denying it.

In our ministry to the sorrowing, we can ease the pain of loneliness. By extending our understanding that they are hurting and assuring them it is normal—they even have a right to feel the pain—

we help them to step out of isolation. Accepting feelings is the first step in working through them. We can never say, "I know just how you feel," because we never do. But our presence and our concern say we do know they feel many confusing emotions and that we are not frightened away.

3

Structures That Serve

Practical assistance, liturgical ministry, long-term support—these gifts we offer the grieving in our midst. Ideally, every Christian community would extend these gifts. Realistically, we have limited resources.

It is far better to attempt less and serve everyone equally well than to plan a wide assortment of services that only reach a few. After all, we do that already.

The first goal of a community ministry to the grieving is to make sure no member grieves alone. Each person touched by death should feel the caring touch of a believing community in at least some small way.

Obviously, a community that averages 100 funerals a year cannot do as much as one that expects a dozen in the same time.

A commitment to reach every grieving person means firm structures with clear responsibilities at every level, a tightly woven network of communication and care that lets no one's need slip through. To be fully effective, the structures we build must provide communication in every direction: to and from the rectory, the grieving persons and the gifted people in ministry.

The rectory

At the core of the network is the rectory, because there the news of a death is first received (although there are exceptions). The dead must be buried within a short time and the hour of the funeral is determined by the availability of church and celebrant.

Usually the call to the rectory comes from a funeral home, though families with special rapport may call the pastoral staff themselves. In any case, the initial contact is an ideal time to introduce the bereavement ministry. Its scope need not be spelled out in detail, but people should be told that a member will be in touch, and for what purpose (to help them plan the funeral liturgy, to offer practical help, simply to express the community's condolences). If the funeral director calls, he can convey the message to the family.

The identification of the family and a few questions about the circumstances of death offer clues to the kind of help urgently needed. Large close-knit families may need less immediate emotional support but a lot more food; a young family with tiny children will need babysitters. A family stricken by tragedy—suicide, sudden or horrible death, the demise of a child—will need the most sensitive persons among us.

Whenever family circumstances are discussed, confidentiality enters the picture. If a man killed in an automobile accident was involved with another woman, the whole world has no right to know. Scandalous gossip can only add to his widow's pain.

The pastor may have the privileged information. The widow may already have come to him for counseling. Certainly he will not communicate his knowledge to the people who are bringing in meals or caring for the baby.

But others need to know. A liturgy-planner left in ignorance might create an awkward moment by suggesting Wisdom 4:7-14 for the funeral—the passage asserts that long life is not to be measured in years but by virtue. The person who offers long-term support needs to be aware that feelings of anger and failure as a wife are probably seething just beneath the widow's tears.

Sharing confidential information presumes a high level of trust. The first leap belongs to the pastoral staff. The rest of us justify that trust with care in our conversations. The grieving need never know that the ministers already knew something it took them months to find the courage to reveal to us. And certainly we must never give careless tongues material for gossip.

The coordinator

Bringing needs and givers together is a time-consuming job. It requires many hours on the telephone and the careful keeping of records to ensure promises are kept. It is a large responsibility. But responsibilities not pinned down are all too often responsibilities unmet.

Someone must accept the duty of overseeing the smooth operation of the ministry effort. The person delegated could be a member of the pastoral staff or a volunteer from the community.

Accessibility is the first qualification. The coordinator must be within easy reach so that the news of a death can be quickly passed to those who will initiate contact with a bereaved family. If the coordinator's availability is interrupted by vacation or personal crisis, a replacement has to step in for the interim.

Notification of a death and information about the family's circumstances is all the coordinator needs to activate the network. He or she may make the first contact with the family personally. Or the coordinator will call someone else to make contact and tend the family's needs.

Usually, the person who makes that first contact will also assume care of the family throughout the grieving period. If there is a practical need, the coordinator might call directly on someone who could provide temporary help. Normally, it is easier to give the contact person an assessment of the needs and to leave the responsibility for coordinating care in his or her hands.

It is a long way from a parked car to the door of a house just visited by death. The journey is easier for someone who already knows the family—a friend, a neighbor, someone whose interests and activities have already opened the door to friendship. If one of the ministers fits that description, not only will the first call be easier, but he or she will not have to work so hard in building a supportive relationship for the months ahead.

To match people, the coordinator needs to know the persons who work in the ministry—their strengths and weaknesses, the circles in which they move. Gifts or flaws will surface only as the ministry develops, and getting to know people always takes time. A wise coordinator will bring at least the core people—those who will be in close contact with the bereaved—together from time to time to deepen the acquaintance.

Groups in ministry

There are many ways to tap a community's gifts. It can be done informally as the need arises, especially in a small parish. In my community, we have found it easiest to define ministry groups by their function. We have perhaps an excessive passion for organization, but we are a fairly large parish (1,300 families) and it works well for us.

We group people by the skills they possess and wish to offer the bereaved: supportive persons, practical helpers and liturgical ministers, with further divisions in the latter two groups.

Designating people for a particular role does not exclude the overlapping ministries. For instance, I may show up to help a family plan a funeral liturgy with coffeecake in hand, fully intending to remain in touch over a long period of time.

What seems a rigid structure gives us the greatest flexibility in meeting the community's needs. Our bereavement ministry is one of 13 groups dedicated to serving human needs. None is subordinate to any other, but each is ready to respond to another's call.

Particularly helpful to the bereaved are the groups that offer child care, meals, drivers and help with household repairs. We make available to families in other kinds of crisis both these ministers and other groups that offer services such as company for shut-ins and part-time nursing care.

Each group's chairperson distributes the calls for help equitably and tries to learn the volunteers' special gifts and friendship ties.

There are other services the bereaved may need: financial assistance, access to job training and counseling for homemakers newly responsible for a livelihood, help with social security or the settling of a simple estate, counseling about burial arrangements. This list could go on, as suggested by your community's needs and resources.

The liturgical ministries, already organized by function in most parishes, comprise another "group of groups" for service to the sorrowing. These include lectors and communion ministers, musicians and ushers. Important too are the community's artists, writers and the unsung persons who mimeograph and fold the programs for the liturgy.

The key element in liturgical ministry to the grieving is the skill of the planning group—people trained to help families plan a funeral they will remember as a good celebration. The liturgy planner can easily coordinate the services of the other ministers.

It does take a lot of people to provide the services just described. For the most part, they minister only to the moment, as friends and neighbors always do. The real core of a bereavement ministry is the group committed to long-term support. They may have all kinds of practical and liturgical skills; but the greatest gifts they bring are simply human skills: compassion, sensitivity, a listening ear.

The group need not be large in number. We began our ministry with a dozen people; since then our number has doubled. In spite of an occasional week when four or five consecutive deaths kept our coordinator very busy, none of us could protest we are overworked. About half of us help plan a funeral liturgy; the rest make contact simply to offer condolences when a family wants no part of planning. All of us are committed to long-term support. Many caring people answer our calls for other kinds of help.

The ministering community

Any ministry, clerical or lay, involves calling forth the gifts of the whole community. Ministry to the grieving is a richly rewarding experience, satisfying the human need to feel needed. But if we satisfy only our need without heightening parish sensitivity, we have not responded very well.

The whole community is called to serve. Without it, the service of a few will still leave people alone and helpless in their grief. The pastoral staff—and through them, the bereavement ministry—can count on notification of death only when the deceased was a member of the community and is to be buried from the parish church.

But death has no respect for parish boundaries. It leaps distance and denominational lines. The death of a partner in a mixed marriage doesn't hurt less if the funeral is held in another church. The death of a grown child across the country is just as unthinkable as the death of the child now asleep upstairs.

These deaths may not cause a ripple in the parish structures, but they do not pass unnoticed in the community. Friends and neighbors know. We cannot plan a liturgy for another parish or another denomination, but we can offer sympathy to the mourners on behalf of the community, or prepare a meal, or walk as friend on grief's bitter journey.

Finally, the bereavement ministry is a force for education. When a person suffers, people are seldom callous and unconcerned. Often they don't know how to help. They avoid the grieving because they feel awkward or confused, or because the answers they give so easily fall short of the questions with which the sorrowing struggle. What do you say to a dead friend's wife months after the funeral? If you speak of your friend and tears well in her eyes, have you made her cry? Grief may be a mystery: a year later, your neighbors are still mourning a dead child. Is that normal?

Helping friends and neighbors understand how the grieving feel brings them into ministry too. When we have really served well, the grieving will be surrounded by understanding and care. We work to put ourselves out of work.

Recruiting

A strong, active bereavement ministry will make itself known without any direct effort. Care speaks softly, but powerfully. Friends and relatives, neighbors and coworkers notice a community's loving response to sorrow. They talk about it. They ask questions. They carry the experience across a city and out of town, back to their own communities.

It doesn't happen overnight. Effective ministry begins when a few dedicated people make a commitment that touches other hearts. Caring, giving people stand out in every parish organization. Many have themselves walked the path of grief; compassion begins with understanding how it feels.

Two currents are moving through our society to draw people into ministry. The first is an interest in death and dying that has been developing since Dr. Elisabeth Kubler-Ross first began to talk to dying patients a decade ago. More and more, grieving people are finding the words to frame their feelings; people yet untouched by sorrow are listening and learning. The second is a deep hunger for real community—not just coffee and doughnuts after the nine o'clock Sunday mass, but ties of love and sharing that give people deep roots in one another.

People active in existing organizations have already demonstrated an interest in community that goes deeper than the surface. Some of them will surely respond to an invitation for more personal involvement with the sorrowing.

The youth group is the most neglected resource in most communities. No other group is looking so hard for evidence of real community care as the young. They need to feel needed, to take their place as contributing community members. They drive, cut grass, babysit, make banners. They are patient with the lonely because they understand the need for love and approval when life's direction is uncertain.

The senior citizens' group has a disproportionate number of people who have been through grief. Those widows and widowers know how long and lonely grief can be. Some of them can bring the precious gift of understanding to the newcomers to sorrow.

The liturgical talent to make funerals memorable can be found on the parish worship team and among the liturgical ministers. Not all lectors, communion ministers, ushers or singers are available for a weekday morning funeral, but some are. The existing rosters are the first channels to explore.

The already involved are not the only people willing to serve. Many people are just not joiners; social organizations fail to attract and hold them. Others are prevented from active participation by life circumstances but would willingly give an occasional hour or a host of everyday skills. Young mothers and housebound senior citizens, for instance, often enjoy making contact with the outside world by telephone. They are a natural complement to the active doers who never have time to make phone calls.

Tapping the resources of the uninvolved requires effort and imagination. Bulletin advertising is seldom effective; there is no substitute for a personal appeal.

A door-to-door campaign is a lot of work, but it is effective. Our ministries program was developed that way. This neighborhood canvass could be tied to a census or survey. A community-wide mailing is also an easy way to reach all the doors. Either approach could explain a bereavement ministry's rationale and purpose and offer a sign-up sheet. A tie-in to a Sunday liturgy when the readings speak of ministry allows people to offer their time and talents with the bread and wine. It's an appropriate occasion to return a sign-up sheet delivered or mailed to the home (extras can be placed in the pews for people with memories like mine).

Training

People who have no concept of grief's length and complexity should not be asked to become intimately involved with the sorrowing; people who do not understand the funeral rite's structure and purpose should not be planning funerals. But skills can be learned. There are people with expertise in liturgy, people already familiar with grief's many faces. Speakers and classes can teach volunteers to help the grieving—and keep them from inflicting further hurt. This book's bibliography (pages 87-89) offers some direction for self-education.

Taking the first step

However well organized the ministry and well trained the volunteers, every death presents a new challenge. We begin all over again with a loss never before experienced, a grief unmatched in all the world. It is always hard to approach someone who has just discovered sorrow. What is there to say or do?

The priorities you establish are the first answer to the question. The primary goal is always to express the community's concern; a simple "I'm sorry" conveys it. The message can be delivered by phone, visit (death suspends formality; even the most meticulous housekeepers forget the dust in their need for comfort) or even by mail. A personal note is a caring touch, even though it leaves the work of building a supportive relationship for later.

Practical assistance may be the best support your community can offer. An accomplished deed speaks the will to help. Then you can ask what *else* you can do, because your concern has become believeable.

If liturgical ministry is the first priority, the family's willingness to become involved with the liturgy is the determining factor in your success. You must explain to them what it means to plan a liturgy—and how choices will be made if they decline. Some families can be led to participation; others will be firm in their refusal. Ministering to the latter's needs will mean listening carefully for hints of their preferences and faith questions, and then planning the best possible liturgy for them.

To initiate planning, make an appointment for a time when the principal mourners will be together. If they have finished with the funeral home arrangements, they will feel freer to turn their attention to the liturgy.

Long-term support begins slowly. You cannot, of course, show up at a stranger's door and say, "I'm here to begin helping you through the months of grief ahead." Most people have no idea what's ahead; they probably wouldn't believe us if we told them.

Gestures of concern, both tangible and intangible, make our understanding apparent and our care believeable. That can take many weeks and repeated calls. At first, we are among many who say, "If there is anything I can do, let me know." A mourner only slowly appreciates the dimensions of the loss, but most of those kind offers will be tacitly withdrawn because people don't expect grief to last more than a few weeks. If we are still there with our offer at that time, a grieving person will believe our concern, even seek our support.

Beginning members in this ministry will need help. If personnel resources allow, two people can make calls together until they both grow comfortable in their role. One person may strike up greater communication with the grieving while the other brings better skills in different areas, such as knowledge of the liturgy. A quiet person may find it easier to visit a stricken family in the company of one more outgoing. But that gift of quiet listening may later prove the perfect catalyst for someone to pour out painfully suppressed feelings.

Paired ministry is a good way to introduce new members to the team, or to showcase the skills of the especially gifted without drawing discomforting comparisons between individuals.

The circumstances of death will influence how we ease new people into ministry. The death of an elderly widowed parent usually creates an atmosphere of peaceful acceptance, especially if a long failure of faculties preceded death—an easy first call. The agony of a suicide or a child's death, on the other hand, can rattle the confidence of even more experienced ministers.

Of course, the Lord has his own plans. When our parish ministry was new, the community's death rate suddenly doubled, and *all* deaths were hard to accept. In our first few months we buried an infant, three young women in their twenties and too many husbands and fathers suddenly dead in their prime. It was not the introduction we would have chosen. We grew quickly in wisdom, experience and sensitivity. We allowed the Lord to move among us with loving power.

Part Two

When Believers
Celebrate Death

4

A Rite Filled with Hope

The end of a life cannot pass unnoticed. It begs to be marked with ritual attention, publicly acknowledged as an event of great significance. Every human society performs traditional rites over its dead.

The familiar motions surrounding death serve the survivors' human need to do one more thing for the person who has moved beyond reach, to actualize this death and let the unthinkable reality begin to penetrate a numbed consciousness.

For Christians, death is a beginning as well as an end, a pause in the passage from earth to eternity. With faith-filled affirmation or with searching questions they bring the dead before the Lord. A loved one's life and death and the grief of those left behind are integrated in the church's funeral rite with Jesus Christ's dying and rising.

The Catholic rite of funerals is a complicated entity because, within its structure, the burial customs of diverse cultures around the world must be incorporated into the one hope of the universal church. In the United States, the rite is celebrated in three "stations," three separate occasions for shared prayer.

Because these three stations comprise one liturgical whole, they should be planned as a unit. The eucharist stands at its center as the peak celebration of Jesus' death and resurrection. All that goes before or after the funeral mass derives meaning and mood from the eucharistic liturgy.

The station in the home

The rite begins with prayerful vigil over the body of the deceased, usually celebrated in the United States in the funeral home during the hours of visitation. The wake's structure is simple and flexible. It is a word service led by a priest, deacon or layperson. When a priest or deacon cannot attend, one of the ministers represents the community and leads the prayer.

The first station consists of an introduction and call to prayer, the praying of a psalm, one or more scripture readings, a homily and prayers of intercession.

The informal setting and the recent loss suggest highly personal prayer. The first reaction to a death is usually a clinging to the memories of life. Families and friends gathered by death exchange their stories and memories of the deceased. Those stories have a place in the first station.

The introduction is essentially a call to prayer. It could incorporate a memory, a favorite poem or prayer of the deceased. It should include an expression of sympathy to the assembled mourners.

The pain of loss is as old as the human race; the cry for God's consolation is as old as faith. The psalms' ancient words link this sorrow with the centuries of prayer that lie behind us. Because it is dear and familiar to Christians of every denomination, Psalm 22/23 ("The Lord is my shepherd") is a favorite choice.

One or more scripture passages introduce the Christian belief in the infinite value and eternal dimension of each believer's life. Both the scripture selections and the homily can reflect the cherished qualities of the dead. The rite prohibits a eulogy at the funeral mass; no such prohibition holds here. The gathering's casual intimacy almost demands that the consolation of memories be shared in the Lord's presence.

The first station concludes with general intercessions and the Lord's Prayer. Again, the setting invites spontaneous, informal prayer, an opportunity for individual participants to speak their hearts' needs.

Music is an appropriate addition to the first station—if there is reasonable hope the gathered crowd will be willing and able to participate. Singing calls for strong leadership, accompaniment and song books.

The celebration of the first station normally replaces the Catholic custom of praying the rosary at the funeral home, but does not preclude it. The rosary could be scheduled at another time within the visitation period.

If there is no visitation, the first station or a simple prayer service should be celebrated at some other time, either when the family gathers at home or when they assemble at the funeral home before the funeral mass. Additional prayers when the casket is closed or at any other time between death and burial are always appropriate.

The station in the church

The second station is the funeral mass, the gathering of the Christian community at the Lord's table to pray for the dead and the living. Because its more complex structure gives the entire rite its shape, I will treat it at length in later chapters (see pages 33-44, 52-59).

The station at the grave

Quiet and simple, the final station is ordinarily celebrated at the cemetery. If the grave has not been blessed, it is blessed at this time. The dead person is commended into God's hands and scripture's consoling words are offered once more. A litany or responsory prayer follows.

If few mourners will accompany the casket to the cemetery, the final commendation takes place at the end of the funeral mass.

In American burial customs, the last amen is spoken over a casket poised on machinery above a covered grave or even in a chapel removed from the gravesite. As people turn to leave, something is left unfinished. They have not really *buried* their dead.

The lost practice of lowering the casket and filling the grave was a brutally real completion of the burial ritual. Many people will protest it is too painful to inflict on the grieving; most cemeteries do not allow it.

But we still need some gesture of final farewell. Mourners can file past the casket and lay a hand on it in goodby, or take a flower from the funeral spray. Or mourners may speak a prayer of farewell, a testimony to the memories they will carry away, or an echo of an earlier parting. Selection of this last gesture should be part of the earlier planning.

Once more, one of the ministerial group may lead the graveside prayer when the clergy cannot be there.

Purpose and movement

The funeral rite has two purposes: to pray for the dead, and to bring comfort and hope to the mourners. The rite has one direction in movement: forward in the footsteps of Jesus Christ, crucified and risen.

The rite begins by acknowledging the pain of loss. It weaves together memory and hope, drawing the life just ended into the mystery of Christ's resurrection. The transition is crystallized in the preface of the mass: "Lord, for your faithful people, life is changed, not ended."

From that point there is no looking back. In the eucharist we are one with the risen Lord. Nothing can separate us from him or from one another, not even death. With trust and faith, we commend our dead into his hands and look forward to our resurrection from sorrow and eventual reunion with those we love.

Prayer for the dead has a very personal dimension, shaped by the memories we cherish, good and bad. The rite acknowledges differing circumstances, with special prayers for those who suffered a long illness, or who died too suddenly or too soon or too young, or who spent their life in service of the gospel.

The needs of the living vary, too. What comforts one person may leave another untouched—prayers, readings, songs. The story of Lazarus speaks powerfully to some; for others it may only raise an agonizing question: "Why does the Lord not return my love to me?" Some are stirred by the rousing strains of "I Will Raise Him Up" with vigorous guitar accompaniment; others are offended, preferring the organ's soft voice.

Shaping a liturgy that makes prayerful sense in the context of this death and speaks to the unique pain of this loss is a natural gesture for the Christian community. Every day, we help one another to pray. On the day of sorrow, our ministry continues.

5

Preparing for Participation

Because it takes time to prepare a good liturgical celebration, the offer of planning help should be extended as soon as the news of death is received, and the planning session scheduled as quickly as possible.

Many people do not understand what it means to plan a liturgy. The suggestion may conjure up memories of liturgies they found distasteful or disturbing. Few understand the flexibility of the funeral rite and the support it offers their prayer.

A detailed explanation of the rite may not help. The burden of planning three stations will discourage someone who has never searched scripture or given serious thought to the structure of the church's prayer.

But the mass is a familiar experience to every Catholic. A well-planned funeral mass may even be a moving event in people's memories. We can help them choose readings whose meaning they understand and whose message is comforting. We can give them the kind of music they like best. We can help them create a funeral that is a personal reflection of a beloved person and a comfort in their sorrow. That is what they should be told.

Some will still refuse, convinced the clergy are trying to shirk their responsibility or protesting the press of decisions thrust on them by the death. This is their right.

A sensitive minister may still discern something of their preferences and their needs. We can put simple questions to them: receiving under both species, choosing lectors, expressing something personal in the prayer of the faithful. The conversation may even remove the threat of the unknown and gently lead them to greater participation in the planning, if only over the phone.

Even when families readily respond to the invitation, the mass should get first attention. Otherwise the planning of the first station may drain energy and the central celebration will suffer. From the planning of the eucharistic liturgy, the needs for the other stations can sometimes be discerned. Or a suggestion inappropriate to the mass can be incorporated elsewhere.

The principal mourners should be involved in the planning session. In an effort to protect a distraught parent, the children may wish to plan the other parent's funeral. But no one needs the consolation of faith more than the person who most feels the loss. It makes little sense to exclude the surviving spouse. We can gently explain we do not intend a further ordeal but a healing experience.

The best time to meet with the family for planning is after the decisions about caskets, visitation and cemetery plots have been made with the funeral director. We are asking for a sizable chunk of time —seldom less than an hour, often three or four hours. The first full day after death is hectic with appointments and phone calls. The following day a heavy lull develops. Because there is little to do but wait, the planning session fits well into that void.

The planners' preparation

Those who volunteer to help plan funeral liturgies accept a leadership role. Some families can make the decisions without the aid of outsiders. All they need is busywork: contacting readers and communion ministers, arranging details. But most will be looking for guidance in this unfamiliar area. We must be prepared to deal with their questions and to anticipate difficulties.

Obviously, we need to bring to their homes all the materials we need. That includes copies of the readings—a Bible, a lectionary, or one of the resources suggested in the bibliography—and the hymnals or songbooks used by the community. A planning sheet or checklist ensures that nothing is overlooked (see chapter 8, pp. 53-54, for a sample). A pencil with an eraser allows people to change their minds, and sample programs or program covers show them what others have created in similar situations.

Familiarity with the funeral rite structure is essential. But we also need to know the human resources that will bring it to life. Who is the celebrant? What musicians will be available for the funeral?

Their limits and their strengths have to be considered in planning decisions.

The hour of the funeral dictates some limits. The choice of lectors and communion ministers is wider for an evening or weekend funeral. The size of the congregation is a factor, determining the number of programs to be printed, the number of communion ministers or ushers needed.

Family circumstances will also play a role. The death may have so shattered them they cannot be pressed to make many decisions. Or the church may have little influence in their lives. Faith questions may have to be explored before any planning is done.

There are pitfalls to avoid, and the first is the temptation to plan the funeral *we* would like. I know the scripture passages that I love; I know the songs that lift my heart. I know what would comfort me if I lost a love, and how I would like my family and friends to celebrate my own death. Before I can serve another's need, I have to let go my preferences. The liturgy I would plan is not theirs.

The human needs of grieving people bring another temptation contrary to the spirit of the funeral rite. Sympathy can suggest bowing to their pressure. Pastoral sensitivity certainly suggest leniency in any gray area. But ultimately the funeral rite is not the prayer of one stricken family but of the whole Christian community. As representatives of the community we have an equal responsibility to the church's concept of the liturgy.

Funerals are for the living

A wag once suggested that of course guitar music should be played at his pastor's funeral. After all, he always said guitars would be allowed in his church only over his dead body. And I'm sure my children will wear their jeans to my funeral to see if I really do sit right up through the coffin lid.

The preferences of the deceased are usually taken much more seriously. Honoring them seems to be the last gesture love can offer, the last service that can be given.

The terrible truth is that the dead don't care. Nothing more can be done for them except prayer. Instead, the liturgy must be planned for the living. Only they can appreciate the experience.

So if Grandpa loved Gregorian chant and the Latin mass and Grandma shared his feelings, a liturgy rich with traditional music and silent prayer will comfort the widow. But if only the grandchildren remain to bury him and they are deeply committed to the charismatic movement, they will find it hard to pray at a liturgy which seems to them cold and rigid. The liturgy Grandpa would have loved will only emphasize the distance death has put between them.

They need the assurance that it is not flagrantly disrespectful to ignore the wishes of the dead. St. Paul offers it: "Eye has not seen, ear has not heard, nor has it so much as dawned on man what God has prepared for those who love him" (1 Corinthians 2:9). If there is music in heaven, nothing in the parish music director's repertoire can begin to compare with it. We are free to plan a liturgy that meets the survivors' needs because the dead are in very good hands.

Some families are as catholic as the church. The range of their tastes covers centuries of Christian tradition. Members of these families are usually sensitive to each other's needs in a time of shared crisis. Our role is to ensure that everyone's needs and preferences are expressed freely. The feelings of the nearest mourner—the husband or wife, the dead child's parents—should normally take precedence, but there is room for compromise. The inclusion of one element of the others' choice, even the patient consideration of their wishes, will result in a loving, balanced liturgy.

The funeral is not a memorial service

At the funeral mass, we remember the gift of a particular life. It is not an anonymous celebration. But we celebrate that life's *fulfillment*. The value of the dead lies beyond all the good they have done. In Christ's resurrection, this life has transcended its previous limits.

Memories are important, and never more so than at the time of death. In memory, we consciously keep all another has been to us. A family gathered to mourn a death spends much time sharing anecdotes and recalling the traits of the dead. We can come to a planning session as strangers and leave with the feeling we have really missed someone special.

Remembering the dead is comforting and healthy, but it is not enough for a Christian celebration. For one thing, memory seldom draws accurately. Holding just to the good gifts obscures reality. If the deceased was truly human, he or she was sometimes irritable, manipulative, unforgiving, selfish and careless. He never remembered anniversaries; with her last breath she interrupted his sentences.

Love, of course, forgives both small annoyances and deep wounds. And that is exactly what Christians celebrate. Love reaches out to us in all our faults and failings. We do not celebrate a person's entry into eternal life because he or she was so good. We celebrate the invitation to life given to all us by a God who is so good. We remember with broken bread and poured wine the death Jesus accepted for us.

Grieving people have much to forgive themselves: the failures large and small, real and imagined in the relationship death has ended. They need to know that God does not abandon us when we are less than perfect.

It is not humanly helpful to idealize the dead, because it may exclude from participation those whose relationship with the dead was strained. The gifts the dead brought are too precious to ignore. But like the gift of bread and wine we bring to the altar, they have become, in Christ's power, something more.

That is what we celebrate. Beyond our understanding, beyond the world we know, the flawed gift we cherished so dearly has been brought to glorious perfection.

6

The Planning Session

You stand at the door of a house just visited by death, ready to help a grief-stricken family plan a funeral liturgy. Where do you begin? The first and most natural gesture is an expression of sympathy.

Some families will look wholly to you for guidance. Others will quickly present something they have been thinking about—a song, prayer or poem, the name of a person they want as lector. A few will even have thought about scripture. Jot down their suggestions and come back to them later.

Because liturgy is prayer, it is best planned in the context of prayer. Share with the family a scripture passage that speaks the Christian view of death. Many of the passages in the rite are ideal. Express your own prayer for the deceased, for the gathered family, for the Spirit's presence in the planning session. Allow a little time for the family members to bring their needs before the Lord and then close the prayer. (If you are uncomfortable with spontaneous prayer, see p. 52 for a simple structure.)

The experience of loss is what educators call "a teachable moment." In the prayerful atmosphere, the next task is catechesis. Explain the rite's twofold purpose: prayer for the dead and comfort for the living. You may want to point out the two pitfalls mentioned in the last chapter (see pp. 35-37). Certainly free the family from any obligation to plan a funeral to the taste of the dead.

Choosing scripture

Now you are ready to begin planning. It may seem illogical, but the point to begin is not the beginning. Start instead with the gospel.

More than any other element, the gospel shapes the liturgy's theme and mood. The homily follows from it and everything else should reflect it.

It takes time and patience to find the one passage that best speaks to this family. Give them time to look at a leisurely pace. In a large group passing books around is clumsy; read the gospels suggested out loud. Or summarize them; stop to read an entire passage when you detect a flicker of interest.

Families will easily narrow the choice to the two or three that echo the personal dimensions of faith and grief. Again allow time to discover the reasons each appeals. Remind them that one or another might serve better at the funeral home or the cemetery.

When the family decides on one passage, be sure that everyone agrees this message comforts. If one person holds back in silence, ask if the passage speaks to his or her grief.

Once the gospel is chosen, the family goes on to select at least one other passage from the New Testament and ordinarily a third passage from the Old Testament or from Acts or Revelation. If they want to keep the funeral quiet and simple, two readings are enough. You can intervene a little more, articulating the theme they have chosen and guiding them toward other passages that echo it. (Donald Senior's *Loving and Dying* is helpful here; see the bibliography, p. 89.)

The readings suggested in the rite do not, of course, embrace the wealth of scripture. The variety offered is good, but circumstances may suggest another selection. One young widow whose husband had fought long with leukemia spoke without hesitation when his struggle—and hers—ended. Her choice for the first reading: Genesis 32:23-31, the story of Jacob's struggle with an angel. The homilist quickly agreed, sensing the possibilities for preaching.

The homilist's agreement is essential; he cannot preach effectively if he does not understand the reasons for the choice of a text. Whenever a passage is selected outside the rite's offerings, submit the choice to the homilist before making any firm promises.

Be sure the family hears the whole passage. Often one verse has struck a responsive chord. Placed in context the line may lose its power. The popular passage from Ecclesiastes ("To everything there is a season") is a good example. The end of a long and loving life may indeed suggest there is "a time to die." But the same passage asserts a time for war, for hatred, for tearing down what has been built.

Once they have chosen the readings, a family has provided the celebrant and the musicians what they need to shape a liturgy to their needs. From this point on, your sensitivity should discern when they are growing exhausted. They have had many decisions to make at this time, and it is best to respect their limits.

Music

Music is the next area for choice. The first question is not what songs to sing but how to underline the action and give real consolation.

The acclamations—the gospel alleluia, the preface acclamation, the memorial acclamation and the great amen—mark the high points of every liturgy. Take it for granted those will be sung; only the choice of musical settings needs consideration.

A sung psalm response after the first reading has two benefits: it underscores our response to God's word and it provides a break that readies the ear to listen better.

The Lord's prayer, the model of all Christian prayer, could be sung at any liturgy. But if the congregation will include a large number of non-Catholics, the decision to sing deserves careful consideration. This is the one prayer all Christians can pray together. The chant melody familiar to Catholics may destroy the unity by excluding others from participation.

Remember the possibility of an instrumental, a solo or a choir piece, especially at the preparation of the gifts or as a recessional. At the offertory, the time people need for reflection on the readings and the homily may be denied them by hurrying into song. If the funeral celebrates one of those tragic deaths that puts a lump in everybody's throat, the end of mass is tinged with terrible finality. Letting someone else carry the burden of song may ease the farewell.

To be appropriate, a song should reflect either the Christian celebration of death or the action of the liturgy. Thus any communion song is appropriate at that point of the mass; any song that expresses hope in resurrection fits anywhere in the liturgy.

Because of your responsibility for the community's prayer, you may sometimes have to say no. Pastoral considerations suggest a degree of flexibility. In any doubtful case you can always argue the family's case to the pastor and the music director. Sometimes a totally inappropriate song might be played before mass as the family comes into church. Borderline selections could become an instrumental at offertory or communion.

The offertory gifts

What about "symbolic" gifts? Remember that bread and wine are already richly symbolic. If an object captures the essence of an ended life, it could be brought to the altar. But if it needs explanation, it does not have the power to express. And if the mourners are not ready to offer freely a loved one's life, the gesture is not honest. The most touching gesture I have seen was the presentation of a rosebud at a baby's funeral. Nothing needed to be said. It spoke clearly of the faith with which the baby's parents had comforted the friends who came to console them. Had it said any less, it would have been empty sentimentality.

Communion meditations

When is a non-scriptural passage an aid to prayer after communion? It should meet three criteria. First, it must not obstruct the liturgy's movement. If it turns back to sorrow, it blocks the forward thrust to the resurrection hope that is the heart of the church's consolation. Second, it must help people to pray. The purpose of the silence after communion is worship. Prayer is more a movement of the heart than of the head; a mini-homily seldom evokes a prayerful response. It should be not only prayerful, but short enough to allow time for hearts to respond. Third, it must have that elusive element called quality. We can argue that many of the official liturgy's prayers fall far short of poetic beauty. That is no excuse to add more words that are clumsy, sing-song or dull. God does not need graceful words, but we do. Funerals should be free of jarring phrases and contrived sentimentality.

The selections eagerly offered by grieving families often fail to meet those criteria. The sentimentality may be hard for the family to handle at that point. Most of us would rather weep with our closest friends rather than in front of a churchful of casual acquaintances. The best way to share a poor selection with the congregation is to print it in the program. Or, it might fit better at the funeral home or as a farewell gesture at the graveside. It may give the homilist an insight into what the mourners need or feel. He could integrate it—or at least its message—into the homily.

The general intercessions

Through the planning session you have been listening to the family's needs. If you have listened carefully, you have probably heard everything that should be in the prayer of the faithful—their doubts and faith, their gratitude and their aching need. Still there may be something that has eluded you.

Ask the family if there is any particular thing they want included. If they ask to craft the prayer, that's fine. But someone with a gift for phrasing prayers should be ready to minister to them.

There is a natural pattern for the general intercessions at a funeral. First we pray for the dead, then for the comfort of the closest survivors. The ended life was the source of special gifts to each of them; the wish to keep something of what was given belongs in their prayer. The loss this death creates for a particularly dependent person (a handicapped child, for instance, or a senile spouse) deserves mention.

If the death has imposed an unusually heavy burden of guilt or anger—as suicide or tragedy does—people should be allowed to pray for healing. Real prayer is honest. It will not expose private anguish if worded with care. And it may be important for the family to know in the months ahead that the most shameful feelings are fit subjects for conversation with the Lord.

Prayers for particular celebrations are excused from the *Sacramentary's* guidelines to pray for the church's needs, the world's and those of all suffering people. But truly Christian prayer always reaches out beyond personal need. The grieving may not be able to reach far, but they can usually pray for those in similar circumstances, for friends and medical professionals who have extended care, or for the needs dear to the heart of the deceased.

If prayer is to remain prayable, it must not preach. The easiest way to turn petitions into mini-homilies is to preface them with *that*. If the widowed Emily is shaky in her faith, the petition, "For Emily, that her faith in the resurrection may be strong," accuses her. Try "Strengthen Emily in faith, Lord," or simply, "For Emily, who loved him."

Sample general intercessions are offered below (see pp. 57-59).

The other stations

If the family has any energy left at this point, explore their preferences for the rite's other stations. Again, the choice of scripture is the first decision; suggest the use of a passage they liked but rejected in favor of another for the funeral mass.

Other rejected choices could be worked into the wake service. If a family member wants to read, the strain of public reading is less at the funeral home. The memories, the poem that would not serve as a communion meditation, could find a place here. If music is wanted, be sure song books will be available.

Encourage spontaneity at the funeral home; the structure is flexible enough to allow free expression. For the graveside, little is needed beyond a scripture passage and a farewell gesture.

The program

A program is a nice remembrance of a funeral tailored to a family's needs and faith. But it is an extra burden for planners, typists and the people who run the mimeograph machine—especially if the funeral planned on Saturday evening is scheduled for Monday morning. Is it worth the extra effort?

A program helps people unfamiliar with the order of services. If the congregation will include people from other denominations, it is a kind gesture of welcome, well worth the effort.

For an entirely Catholic congregation, it may be unnecessary. Then it is simply a gift of remembrance from a loving community. Its preparation depends on the available resources.

Even if the resources are slim and the congregation homogenous, a program gives a family a way to share a text unsuitable for reading publicly. If a family will have no other opportunity to extend thanks and appreciation for a communal expression of sympathy, a program may be the only vehicle for that expression.

Attractive covers are commercially available and can be kept in stock. Or, the community's artistic talents could design a cover. And the family's artistic gifts should be considered. A drawing for a program may be a talented grandchild's special gift to both grandparents, the one who has died and the one left behind.

The program's contents should be the essential minimum. Anything meant to be heard should not be printed: the readings, the prayers, the words of a solo song.

Anything that gives direction in an unfamiliar setting should be included. The ecumenical congregation will find it helpful to know when to sit and when to stand. The symbols used in the rite (pall, candle, incense) might be explained for any congregation except the most liturgically aware.

In the reproduction of words and music, copyright laws must of course be respected. Music easily accessible in the hymnal should not be duplicated in the programs.

Sample programs are included below, pp. 55-56.

7

People in Ministry

The funeral was for one of those we call too young to die—a man in his 40's felled by a heart attack. Every eye in the church was on the slim teenager who stepped to the lectern. She hesitated for just a moment as she gazed at her father's casket, then she began to read—beautifully.

Afterwards, her friends were filled with praise. "I couldn't have done it," more than one was heard to say. Their elders too were touched, moved by the girl's grand effort.

It takes courage to read at the funeral of someone very close, to face dry-eyed the casket of someone on whom you were dependent in many ways. It takes strength to look into the pained faces of the people you love best and maintain your composure. People who can do it are an inspiration to all of us; we draw courage from them. They satisfy our need to see the finest human effort.

But why should the stricken serve *our* need? What happens the next week, the next month, when that teenager begins to realize her father is lost to her for the rest of her life? She has already created an image before everyone she knows; she is brave and strong. To whom does a child-woman dare to reveal the terrible weakness she feels?

Suppose, though, the scene is played thirty years later. Her father is an old man, gifted beyond the three score and ten we count a full life. And she is a middle-aged woman. If the relationship between them was good, their love has grown, not diminished. But the *relationship* itself has changed. No longer are they dependent child and protective parent, but adults together—or their roles have even reversed and it is the father who has grown dependent on the child.

To read is an easier task. If the ministry of the word is part of her calling, if she has been the source of strength to the rest of the family in her father's last illness and cared for the old man's every need, no one is better suited to read at the funeral.

So what do you say to the family member who wants to read at a funeral?

The rite suggests it is desirable for the deceased's relatives and friends to take an active part in the liturgy. But there is a difference between participation and ministry. The congregation at any liturgy participates in a very active sense. There are no spectators at mass.

Ministry presumes qualifications. Public reading of scripture demands skill in lifting the word from the page and letting it live. A person must have experience with a microphone and ease before an audience. A funeral will call on emotional qualifications beyond what the most deeply stricken can offer. No one in a dependent relationship with the deceased should ever feel *obliged* to assume any public ministerial role. We are the ones who should be ministering to them.

Often, rather than a sense of obligation, what prompts people to volunteer is a desire to offer one last gift to the dead, to do one more thing for the person who has moved beyond all need for their services. It would be heartless for us to refuse that need; but we must be sure they understand the difficulties. If they have never read publicly before, they need to know what the view is like from the lectern. Reading in public the first time is hard. Reading at a funeral is always hard. A vivid description of the scene—the coffin, the tear-stained faces, the expectation in the eyes of the congregation—may convince them they are not up to it after all.

If the need to give outweighs the hazards, help them do it well. For lectors, that means providing copies of the readings for advance study, finding time for practice before the microphone, being sure the place in the *Lectionary* is plainly marked and providing clear cues. As a last resort, we can offer the comfort of knowing a competent lector is in a prearranged spot, watching and ready to take over at a last-minute nod if panic strikes.

The same arrangement should be made for every visible role in the liturgy. Will the close friend who has offered to sing suffer a constricted throat? Will the grandchildren who are servers in another parish be confused in an unfamiliar church? Does the friend the family suggests for the ministry really feel up to it, or just reluctant to refuse?

Presenting the gifts of bread and wine is a public gesture most families can manage, but even that shouldn't be taken for granted. A stricken family may be on the verge of breaking down completely; they may not wish to expose themselves unnecessarily.

A sense of perspective

We run a risk when we begin to guide people in and out of ministry for the funeral liturgy. We are only supplementing the service of those who have ministered for years in the parish. We need to keep our ministry to the grieving in perspective.

Some participants in the funeral are strangers to the parish: they do not know where the restrooms are, or where to take a crying child, how to move at communion time. They should be greeted at the door, put at ease and freed in mind and heart for participation.

Parishioners who attend have been here for funerals before, and they know we will seat the family in the front pews. Because they thoughtfully leave a lot of room for them, we can ask them to move up closer where the grieving family can see them and find comfort in their nearness.

Several people in the grieving ministry may have to serve as ushers. If the regular Sunday ushers are there to help, they may need coaching on the special needs of funeral congregations. They may take a new sense of their ministry back to the Sunday liturgy.

Working with celebrants

The celebrant cares. He is sometimes busy or tired or distracted, but he cares. That's why our ministry is needed, so he can do well what he has dedicated himself to.

The best help is good communication, and the planning sheet is one of the tools we use. Every possible detail is filled out to provide a clear and accurate roadmap for the liturgy.

But the planning sheet is only the first clue to the liturgy's shape. The reasons behind a family's choices can be just as important to the preacher as the choices themselves. Does the strong resurrection theme reflect a family's certain faith—or their struggle to believe?

Where families have chosen readings not offered in the rite, the celebrant needs to understand why. But there are limits to everyone's tolerance. The thinking that led to a certain decision may bend those limits to the breaking point. The celebrant has a responsibility for the community's faith, and he has to exercise his responsibility *as he sees it*. He may sometimes have to say no.

Anything in a family's mood or circumstances that may be significant in the course of the liturgy should be reported to him. Who are these sorrowing people; who was the person for whom they mourn? Ideally, of course, he knows the family well. Even so, even though he may have been in close touch with them throughout the fatal illness and is sensitive to the stresses, he may not know about Aunt Ada's crippling arthritis. Knowing, he would take communion to her in her pew. Better to tell him something he already knows than to risk uncertainty.

Last-minute surprises should be avoided at any cost. Presiding at a funeral is fraught with difficulties. No one besides the celebrant is always before the congregation; no one else carries their dependence so heavily. It demands his full attention and his prayerful preparation. The time for working out details or disagreements is long past when the hearse arrives at the church door.

Visiting celebrants create special problems. They come as friends or relatives of the grieving; their role is precious and they deserve respect. Long acquaintance may have given them unique insight into a family's problems and needs. They will rightfully feel resentful if presented with a liturgy plan at the last minute.

Whenever possible, contact a visiting celebrant before the planning session. He may not know the bereavement ministry exists; he is hard at work on the homily, choosing a theme for the liturgy long before he arrives at the church. His advice may be very helpful in guiding the family through liturgy plans. He deserves the same careful communication as the local clergy.

Occasionally there are priests less than enthusiastic about lay participation in liturgical planning. The ministry may have to be justified in this fashion: "Father, we represent our community's concern for the bereaved. Not everyone has a friend like you to plan the liturgy and in any case we feel it is important for the people of the parish to be personally involved—part of our response to the Lord's command to love one another. The planning session gives us a good opportunity for beginning a relationship of long-term support." When all else fails, call on the pastor for help. Ask him to acquaint the stranger with the ministry team when funeral arrangements are first made.

Working with musicians

The music director knows the limits of the congregation, the choir, the cantor. From the beginning, it is wise to tap this rich resource. He or she not only cares about the quality and appropriateness of the music, but also its suitability to a particular community's musical ability.

If the music director is willing to compile a list of suggested music for funerals, it could serve as an aid to planners. A family with no preconceived choices will find it easier to look over a list than to thumb through a hymnal. Even a tape that includes choir or solo pieces could be prepared. It would spare us the embarrassment of trying to carry a melody at the planning session.

The music director has the full responsibility for a parish music program, including the rehearsal of a volunteer choir or the recruitment of cantors. If a cantor is a close friend or particular choice of a bereaved family, pass the word on quickly. It is easy to ask that person to serve; it is embarrassing to call a cantor already contacted and try to explain why his or her services are not needed after all.

Like the celebrant, the musician needs an early copy of the planning sheet and an explanation of the reasons for any unusual selection. In keeping with his or her responsibility, the music director may veto something alien to the community's faith. A family who insists on an unjustifiable choice should be aware of that possibility.

The musician needs help to be sensitive to the mood the family wishes to prevail in the liturgy. If, at some point, he finds it necessary to insert an extra piece of music and reaches for an upbeat favorite, it might be jarring to people seeking quiet, low-key comfort. Similarly, the musician should be aware of the family's preference for absolute silence at any particular point. If an unfamiliar piece is really important to a sorrowing family, it is worth the effort to find and learn the music.

Until the kingdom unfolds in all its glory, we have to work with what we have. If the music director insists a piece is beyond the capabilities of choir or instrumentalist, that's not rigidity; it's an admission of human inadequacy and deserves sympathetic acceptance.

Among Catholics, still growing accustomed to congregational singing, music has been a point of division. Parish musicians often bear the brunt of conflicting expectations. They don't play the old songs anymore; they never play anything new; they play too slow, too fast, too loud, too low and too high—all at once, apparently! People with strong feelings may demand that someone else play at a funeral, but there's good reason to resist that request—gently, of course.

First, parish musicians are part of the community. They share the community's concern for the sorrowing and the call to serve. They have pledged their availability—something the musicians the family prefers may not be able to offer.

More importantly, the music director's willingness to accommodate a family's taste on a sad occasion may do more to heal the bitter estrangement than a thousand explanations of how musical decisions are made.

Working with funeral directors

Funeral directors are in business to serve. If they don't meet the expectations of the grieving, business falls off. No other industry depends so heavily on referrals from individuals and parishes.

Some years ago, Jessica Mitford published an attack on the funeral industry, entitled *The American Way of Death*. Since then, funeral directors have taken a hard look at their practices and redoubled their efforts to meet real needs. Some are even beginning to offer long-term support.

The Christian community must now ask how much of our responsibility we have shunted to their shoulders, and how we can resume our care in partnership with them.

The bereavement ministry can help funeral directors to provide better service in many ways. Taking liturgy planning out of their hands is an obvious relief. Even more, we can acquaint them with the expectations of the parish community.

For instance, the funeral directors in my part of Cincinnati habitually seat the family in the front pews on the right side of the church. Unlike neighboring churches, our lectern is on the left side. Readers and homilists found it difficult to maintain eye contact with the principal mourners. In our work with funeral directors, we began to ask them, one by one, to move families across the aisle.

Other practices we have gently challenged are the seating of pallbearers and the distribution of memorial cards. Lining pallbearers up in the front row blocks the contact between the family and the celebrant or lector. If they sit on the aisle beside their families they can still move in and out easily.

Of all the ways to distribute memorial cards, the least desirable is during the liturgy. If the cards must be distributed at mass, they are given to people as they enter or leave—and we are glad to help.

Funeral directors help our ministry. Often, they are the first to introduce us to the family. Their kind remarks do much to give us credibility and ease us into hesitant lives. A call to the funeral director often yields information lacking to the rectory. They know at which family member's home the people have gathered; they know when the decisions about caskets are complete; they sense who is taking the leadership role within a family.

Funeral directors have to respect confidentiality, too. In the ministry's beginning, or in contacting a funeral home that does not often serve your community, you may meet with polite refusal to reveal any information about a grieving family. Referring the matter to the rectory readily distinguishes ministry from attempted exploitation.

No one's care is unimportant when people are hurting. The better we work together with everyone who has contact with the grieving, the better we express in our ministry the love that characterizes a Christian community.

8

A Sampler for Planners

Nothing I offer can substitute for the gifts of your community members. But if you are uncertain about the shape of prayers or programs, the following may serve as models.

Prayer with a grieving family

Before beginning to plan the funeral liturgy, invite the family to join you in prayer:

"You have my prayers in your sorrow. I need your prayers, too; I feel utterly helpless in the face of your loss. Before we begin to plan the funeral liturgy, let's take a minute to put ourselves in the Lord's hands, remembering the promise his apostles have passed down to us."

Read 1 Thessalonians 4:13-18 or John 6:37-40 and pause for a moment of silent reflection.

"Lord Jesus, we do believe that you died and rose again. We do believe that you will raise us to new and lasting life. Help us cling to our belief in this time of sorrow. Lift our eyes to the hope you offer as we struggle to celebrate all that has been and all that we hold in faith is yet to come.

"Comfort the (last name) family gathered here in sorrow:" (name the people individually).

"Let them keep all their lives the gift (the dead person) gave."

Name the particular needs you know, and invite the family members to add their petitions.

"We have no memory, no hope that is greater than you, Lord Jesus. No one else can dry our tears. You are Lord of the living and of the dead, now and forever. Amen."

The Planning Sheet

Funeral of:_____Date/time:_____

Celebrant:_____

Planner:_____Phone:_____

Principal mourners:_____

_____

_____

Lectors:_____

Distributors:_____

Musicians:_____

Servers:_____

Processional song:_____

First reading:_____

Response:_____Sung___Recited____

Second reading:_____

Alleluia verse:_____

Gospel:_____

Homily suggestions:_____

_____

_____

_____

Offertory procession: yes ( ) no ( )

Gift bearers:_____

Additional gifts:_____

Offertory song:_____

Communion: Bread only ( ) Both species ( )

Planning Sheet, page 1

Communion song:_____

Recessional:_____

Other music:_____

_____

Other arrangements (banners, etc.):_____

_____

Copies attached: Intercessions ( ) Communion meditation ( )

Notes for the celebrant:_____

_____

_____

_____

Notes for musicians:_____

_____

_____

Wake service:_____

_____

_____

_____

_____

_____

_____

Graveside service:_____

_____

_____

_____

_____

_____

Planning Sheet, page 2

Page 1

Mass of Christian Burial

for

Janet Anderson

April 27, 1980

Page 2

On the day of her baptism, the saving waters flowed over Janet and she was clothed in the white garment of innocence. As her body is brought into church, she is once more sprinkled with holy water and the white garment of God's children laid over her casket. The paschal candle, symbol of the risen Lord, goes before her.

Please stand as we begin our celebration of Janet's entry into new life by singing #8 in Glory and Praise, "Be Not Afraid."

Please be seated as we listen to the word of the Lord. The first reading is Wisdom 3:1-9.

We sing our response to Psalm 27: "The Lord is my light and my salvation."

The second reading is 2 Corinthians 5:1, 6-10.

We stand to acclaim the gospel of Jesus as we sing, "Alleluia!"

The gospel is John 11:17-27.

Please be seated for the homily.

As we pray for all our needs, our response is: "Lord, hear us."

Janet's children will present the bread and wine to be used in this eucharistic celebration. Father Reilly will incense the gifts and the body that once housed Janet. Our prayer is that all these gifts will rise like the sweet-smelling smoke and be graciously received by God.

Please stand as Father invites us to join in prayer:

Page 3

Father: "The Lord be with you."

All: "And also with you."

Father: "Lift up your hearts."

All: "We lift them up to the Lord."

Father: "Let us give thanks to the Lord our God."

All: "It is right to give him thanks and praise."

And we sing together: "Holy, holy, holy Lord,/God of power and might,/Heaven and earth are full of your glory./Hosanna in the highest!/Blessed is he who comes in the name of the Lord./Hosanna in the highest!"

Catholics kneel for the eucharistic prayer; others may be seated. As Father invites us to proclaim the mystery of our faith, we sing: "Dying you destroyed our death,/ rising you restored our life./Lord Jesus, come in glory!"

At the end of the eucharistic prayer, we sing our "Amen" and stand to pray the words Jesus taught us: the Lord's Prayer.

The exchange of a handshake or a kiss of peace expresses our concern for one another in this and every sorrow.

As communion is distributed, we sing #13 in Glory and Praise: "Earthen Vessels."

Our response to the concluding litany is "Lord, save your people."

We conclude our celebration by singing #27 in Glory and Praise: "In Him We Live."

Sample program for an ecumenical congregation

56

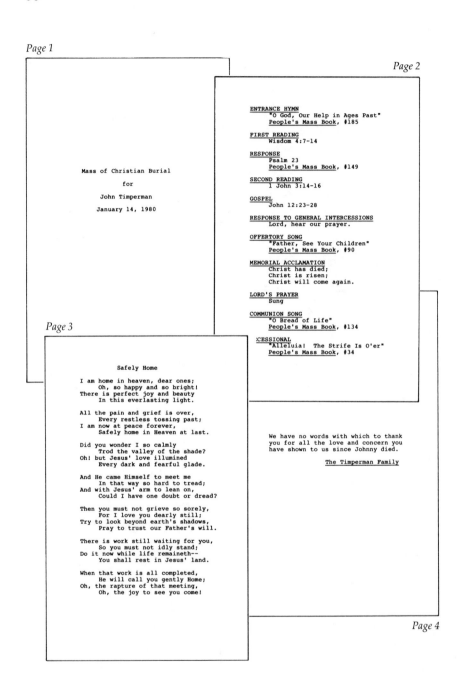

Page 1

Page 2

Mass of Christian Burial

for

John Timperman

January 14, 1980

ENTRANCE HYMN
"O God, Our Help in Ages Past"
People's Mass Book, #185

FIRST READING
Wisdom 4:7-14

RESPONSE
Psalm 23
People's Mass Book, #149

SECOND READING
1 John 3:14-16

GOSPEL
John 12:23-28

RESPONSE TO GENERAL INTERCESSIONS
Lord, hear our prayer.

OFFERTORY SONG
"Father, See Your Children"
People's Mass Book, #90

MEMORIAL ACCLAMATION
Christ has died;
Christ is risen;
Christ will come again.

LORD'S PRAYER
Sung

COMMUNION SONG
"O Bread of Life"
People's Mass Book, #134

:CESSIONAL
"Alleluia! The Strife Is O'er"
People's Mass Book, #34

Page 3

Safely Home

I am home in heaven, dear ones;
    Oh, so happy and so bright!
There is perfect joy and beauty
    In this everlasting light.

All the pain and grief is over,
    Every restless tossing past;
I am now at peace forever,
    Safely home in Heaven at last.

Did you wonder I so calmly
    Trod the valley of the shade?
Oh! but Jesus' love illumined
    Every dark and fearful glade.

And He came Himself to meet me
    In that way so hard to tread;
And with Jesus' arm to lean on,
    Could I have one doubt or dread?

Then you must not grieve so sorely,
    For I love you dearly still;
Try to look beyond earth's shadows,
    Pray to trust our Father's will.

There is work still waiting for you,
    So you must not idly stand;
Do it now while life remaineth--
    You shall rest in Jesus' land.

When that work is all completed,
    He will call you gently Home;
Oh, the rapture of that meeting,
    Oh, the joy to see you come!

We have no words with which to thank
you for all the love and concern you
have shown to us since Johnny died.

The Timperman Family

Page 4

A program using a poem unsuitable for the liturgy

The general intercessions

Write the whole prayer, the introduction (which usually reflects the readings) and the closing prayer as well as the petitions. The celebrant is not required to use them, but it may be a relief to him not to have to "wing it."

For a sudden death

There are many rooms in our Father's house. As its doors close behind George, let us join our voices in prayer.

> With sorrow, we bid goodbye to George. Welcome him tenderly to your house, Lord, we pray.
>
> With concern, we pray for his wife and children. Heal the wound of unexpected loss, Lord, we pray.
>
> With thanksgiving, we remember George's constant thoughtfulness. Extend his concern through all our lives, Lord, we pray.
>
> With new understanding, we pray for all who grieve. Fill their lives with caring people, Lord, we pray.
>
> With deep hurt, we struggle with anger against this death, this waste. Lead us to forgiveness, Lord, we pray.

Father, we are not ready to face this loss, and so we bring our pain to you. Fill our hearts with the hope you hold out to us in the death and life of your Son. In his name we pray, Jesus Christ, our Lord forever. Amen.

For a suicide

Surely the Lord holds all his people fast in his love. With confidence, let us pray.

> We bring Sheila before you, broken and defeated. In your mercy, raise her, Lord, we pray.
>
> We bring you Eric, her husband, whose love could not hold her. Fill his heart with your love, Lord, we pray.
>
> We bring before you our sense of failure and guilt. Lift our sorrow from us, Lord, we pray.
>
> We bring you all our memories of brighter days. Give them power to outshine this darkness, Lord, we pray.

We bring before you all the despair of this wounded
world. Raise us all in new hope, Lord, we pray.

Father, pity Sheila in her pain; pity us in ours. We pray in the name
of your Son, Jesus Christ, our hope in all despair and our Lord
forever and ever. Amen.

At the end of a long, full life

My friends, living and dead are united in the love of Jesus Christ. Let
us place all our needs in his hands.

Look tenderly on Lee, who stands in your presence, Lord. Let
him find joy in the glory that is yours from all eternity, we
pray.

Look tenderly on Ellen, whom we remember with love, Lord.
Heal the pain of separation, and bring husband and wife
together again, we pray.

Look tenderly on the family drawn so close by Lee's need,
Lord. Let the care they gave live on in their hearts, we pray.

Look tenderly on the nurses who gave so freely, Lord. Touch
the emptiness in their hearts with your love, we pray.

Look tenderly on those who age in loneliness, Lord. Open
our hearts to their need and consecrate our gifts to their
service, we pray.

Father, we give thanks for the many touches of your love we felt in
Lee's long life. Lift from us every trace of sorrow, that we may
rejoice with him in the everlasting love of your Son, Jesus Christ,
our Lord. Amen.

At the end of a long illness

The Lord has promised that those who trust in him shall find peace
and joy. Let us turn to him in this sorrow and pray.

For Maria, released now from pain, we ask wholeness and
everlasting life, as we pray to the Lord.

For the family who watched and prayed at her bedside, we
ask comfort and peace, as we pray to the Lord.

For the doctors and nurses who gave such tender care, we
ask every blessing, as we pray to the Lord.

For the persecuted for whom she offered her pain, we ask justice and freedom, as we pray to the Lord.

For ourselves, baffled by the mystery of suffering, we ask understanding and faith, as we pray to the Lord.

Father, we stand before your Son's cross. In his name we pray for comfort. In his death he gathered all our pain; in his glorious resurrection he holds out the promise of everlasting joy. In his name we pray, Jesus Christ, our brother and our Lord. Amen.

For someone very young

The Lord invites us to place our burdens in his hands. With trust, let us pray.

For Nancy, whose life was short but precious, let us pray to the Lord.

For Tom and Alice, who nurtured her growth, let us pray to the Lord.

For the neighbors and friends who weep in sympathy, let us pray to the Lord.

For parents with aching hearts all over the world, let us pray to the Lord.

For ourselves, signs of promises unfulfilled, let us pray to the Lord.

Father, in your hands we place Nancy, still young and full of promise. Hear the prayers we make in the name of Jesus Christ, in whom every promise is fulfilled beyond all our expectations. He is the Son you gave for love of us, our brother and our Lord. Amen.

Part Three

Walking
with the Grieving

9

Grief's Journey

Grief is not something one ever really "gets over." The loss remains a fact for a lifetime, like the loss of a leg. And the old pain may suddenly begin to throb years later, without warning or apparent reason.

But in the beginning, to continue the analogy, grief is like learning to walk without a leg. When at last the loss is integrated, the missing toes no longer throb and the person moves without conscious effort —at least, most of the time.

Nothing about grief is simple; its course is long and circular, its description elusive. It is less a feeling than an experience, less an emotion than a whirlpool that pulls us deeper and deeper until escape seems hopeless.

There is no tidy progression, no sequence of stages to tick off on the way to recovery. C.S. Lewis, chronicling his grief after his wife's death, described it this way in *A Grief Observed:* "Grief is like a long valley, a winding valley where any bend may reveal a totally new landscape. As I've already noted, not every bend does. Sometimes the surprise is the opposite one; you are presented with exactly the same sort of country you thought you had left behind miles ago. That is when you begin to wonder whether the valley isn't a circular trench."

But if no clear roadmap can be drawn, there are features common to almost every person's journey through that winding valley. Very briefly, numbness, anger, guilt and depression are the commonest experiences of grief.

Numbness

Death, whether long expected or surprisingly sudden, numbs survivors with an emotional anesthesia. It often finds expression as disbelief: "I can't believe she's really dead."

Some people describe it as a divorce from reality. They go through the motions of receiving condolences and burying their dead as though they were spectators watching from a great distance, or robots who move without feeling anything, their tears frozen in a hard inner lump.

The reality of death often doesn't even begin to penetrate consciousness until a week or two after the funeral. When the last call has been received and the last thank-you note written, the ensuing silence echoes with the absence of someone loved. When the threads of interrupted living must at last be picked up, the missing of a vital piece is soon apparent.

The painful permanence of the loss unfolds slowly. But reality can crash in at unexpected moments. Waking in the night, a woman turns to touch a husband—and he is not there. The habits of years are shattered, one by one: this toy will not delight a dead child on the next birthday; that seasonal task will not be performed by a dead spouse.

It may take months for the full reality of loss to dawn, years before the loss ceases completely to be a surprise. Meanwhile, a person has been coping from day to day in merciful numbness. When the anesthetic wears off, the pain throbs unbearably. To the surprise of the bereaved and the alarm of their friends, their situation has grown worse instead of better. In the first months after death, they have been on a long downhill slide they did not recognize. Grief works to accept an unacceptable, incomprehensible reality.

Numbness can be nurtured; and when it is, its name is denial. The comfort of alcohol or brightly-colored pills, a plunge into frantic activity, a move to flee the memories of home, burying oneself in the work to be done—there are many ways to hold the hurt at a distance.

Anger

It's nice to have someone to blame when things go wrong. On the job or at home, we would much rather speak of another's failure. Even where our charges are patently false, someone must bear the brunt of our frustration: a coworker, a spouse, a child, even the family pet. Logic has nothing to do with it.

When life goes so wrong that a person significant to us has died, anyone at all can be held responsible. Anger wears the semblance of logic. We direct it at the doctor who made a wrong diagnosis or at the driver of the other car. Or we can just as easily unleash it on innocent bystanders: the child who spills, the careless clerk, the friend whose husband is alive.

God is not exempt from our anger. He alone holds power over life and death; who better to blame? God conceived the plan that robbed a dear one of life and left the survivor alone and helpless.

Most painfully, we feel anger against the dead. They are tried and found guilty of desertion. Feelings of love and anger struggle with each other. When anger wins, shame sets in—what an awful way to feel about the dead!—and adds to the burden of guilt. Or anger is suppressed and denied, too shameful to admit.

Anger is a two-edged sword. Contained, it is corrosive: smothered anger causes a host of physical ailments, from insomnia to ulcers. Unleashed, it wounds the innocent and damages relationships. Sooner or later, its accusations must be met and answered.

Guilt

Guilt is anger turned inwards against the self. Like anger directed against another, it ranges from the wholly logical to the wholly illogical.

None of us is as kind, sensitive or thoughtful as we would like to be. Nowhere do we fail more often than in our relationships with those closest to us. They are easily taken for granted. With them we don't have to maintain the image we present to the rest of the world.

When death takes someone close, it is too late to change our ways. When death is sudden, there is no time for apologies. Survivors are left with a lot of unfinished business: quarrels unresolved, words of love forever unspoken.

Not all the guilt is real. We all have 20/20 hindsight; we would do better if we knew the outcome. But in the messy business of daily living, we do the best we can—and thank God for those with whom we don't have to pretend perfection.

The failure to prevent a death imposes guilt, too. People blame themselves for what they could not possibly foresee. If the weary mother had not told her child to go outside for a while, he would not have been in the car's path. If the husband had noticed sooner how tired his wife looked, the fatal illness might have been diagnosed in time. "If only" is this guilt's haunting refrain.

Even a moment's relief from grief can cause guilt. A pleasant evening brings laughter and forgetfulness—and a sudden charge of infidelity against oneself when memory returns.

Where anger rages or guilt weighs, the work of grief is forgiveness.

Depression

Depression wears many faces, from the restless blues of a rainy day to the gray hopelessness that prompts thoughts of suicide. The depression that accompanies grief can wear all of them: the conviction, at the slightest mishap, that all control over life is lost; the heavy pall hanging over the Christmas holidays; the sleepless night with waking to fresh pain; the loss of hope that grief will ever end; the temptation to find in death the one lost in life.

Depression paralyzes. The simplest, most ordinary task becomes an insurmountable obstacle. Surviving each day is difficult; looking forward to tomorrow is impossible. To cry out for help, even to take an outstretched hand, is an unmanageable effort. Grief works to find new meaning and purpose in a life that has been totally disrupted.

Profound disruption

Death disrupts a survivor's life in more ways than can be imagined. From infancy, we see ourselves in the mirror of important relationships. We know ourselves as wise or witty or loving because another has discovered those qualities in us.

It does not matter that a relationship is not good. Even in a troubled marriage or a turbulent parent-child relationship, basic self-concepts are formed and maintained: I am right, I am abused, I am the giving one.

It is not romantic metaphor to say something of the self dies with a loved one. The surest mirror is gone; a new sense of self, a new feeling of wholeness must now build slowly. But there is no space for calm and collected self-assessment. It is more like trying to rebuild a tornado-leveled house while the winds still blow. The meaning of the rest of the world is just as badly shaken. Home, hospital, automobile accident, wife—hundreds of ordinary words are colored with new meaning. Plans for the future have been stolen, shattered. From one end of life to the other, there is reason to feel cheated.

A difference in degree

Grief's elements are many, but they are common to the experience of most bereaved people. Particular circumstances bring some of them into stronger play. A suicide, for instance, leaves extraordinary feelings of failure and guilt. It appears as a profound rejection and it sparks anger. Or a long illness before death may provide the time to heal old rifts and leave survivors with little sense of guilt. Some people seem born with an innate optimism that fights off depression —or makes its stranglehold harder to understand.

10

Accepting the Limits

If grief is complex, then it seems prudent to hesitate before undertaking a ministry to the sorrowing—as we would hesitate to take apart a complicated piece of machinery. There is much we can do to help the grieving. But there is more we cannot do. If we do not first make peace with our helplessness, we can never fully enter into the possibilities.

Coming to terms with death

None of us has completely accepted the reality of death. The imagination flatly refuses to picture final, lifelong separation from those we love best. When someone's arrival is delayed beyond plausible explanation, icy fingers may grip our hearts, but we label our thoughts *unthinkable*.

We will, if pressed, acknowledge we will die someday—but the emphasis falls on *someday*. Faced with the certainty of death within the hour, we would protest our need for just a little time to say goodbye, to finish what we are doing, to set our affairs in order.

Death in old age is a little more acceptable. But how old is old? Older than I am! Even the humorist Ogden Nash notes in a serious moment, "But the old men know when an old man dies."

We are right to resist death. That's only good theology. Through all of revelation, our God has displayed his will for life. Death, says the Genesis story, was not his plan for his creation. The book of Wisdom repeats the theme: "God did not make death, nor does he rejoice in the destruction of the living" (1:13). In the resurrection of Jesus Christ, death has been defeated. It is God's victory—and ours.

Still, we live somewhere between Eden and the second coming; the tension of the time between holds us fast. If we abandon hope, we deny our faith; if we deny the pain, we refuse our own experience. Our faith rests in one who came to Easter only by way of Calvary. We proclaim there is meaning to be revealed beyond suffering, not that suffering has ceased to exist.

The balance between faith's bright promise and life's dark pain constantly challenges ministry to the grieving. Meeting another's pain and knowing our helplessness is difficult but unavoidable.

We cannot remove the pain

Human sympathy demands that we try. Funeral home conversation is full of the effort. The cliches are repeated: "You had many good years together." "You're young; you'll have other children." "It's God's will."

The cliches may speak real conviction. They are offered with the best of intentions. But they deny the reality of the loss, the irreplaceable quality of the dead person.

The desire to remove the pain is not wholly selfless. It hurts to see someone we care about suffer. If we could erase the pain, *we* would be happier—free from regret, from the burden of listening, from guilt for having living wives and husbands and children.

The human wish to escape another's sorrow erodes the support grieving people receive at first from family and friends. No one wants to hear again and again the story of the fatal accident; no one wants to see tears fall time after time. The grieving who speak their sorrow are avoided. They have an illness which is contagious, and no one wants it.

The grieving who do not speak their feelings are left to sort through them alone. We can listen. We can help—to a point.

We cannot manage another's grief

With profound insight into human behavior, Jesus spoke about sighting the speck in our brother's eye. It is always easier to diagnose from the outside than from within, whether the problem be the roots of a quarrel, a child's bad grades or the workings of grief. It is easier to recognize another's avoidance of death's reality than our own wish for grief's conclusion. It is easier to say, "You ought to get out of the house," than to sit and share with another depression's crushing weight.

Knowing grief's patterns is the proverbially dangerous little bit of knowledge. Recognition means helping another name the inner chaos, but there is no magic power in the name of a feeling. Naming a disease is only the first step in its cure. Whether stroke or brain tumor causes paralysis, it must be overcome slowly and patiently in the physical therapy room. Just so, everyone must work through grief at his or her own pace. The best help we can offer is to adjust our stride and walk beside the sorrowing.

We cannot solve every problem

Grief complicates life. A loss can cause many problems: financial difficulties, a child's relapse to bedwetting. But not every problem is death's fault. A teenager's dependence on drugs is not helped by a parent's death; but death is not responsible. An irascible old man may be angry about the loss of his wife—or just finding new targets for the abuse she absorbed.

Unsolved problems and grief aggravate each other. Certainly we need to be sensitive to the stresses tearing at a person's life. But our task is to help the person carry the burden of grief. If solutions to other problems can be found along the way, so much the better. We haven't failed if they aren't. We will be disappointed if we believe our concern will heal *every* wound.

Neither can we realistically expect to be equally supportive to every member of a bereaved family. Even people in close relationships cannot be everything to each other all the time. A family in grief sometimes has conflicting needs, often differing needs. A child's need for attention goes untended while a parent is sunk in deep depression. The dead child's father may seek forgetfulness in a festive evening when his wife wants to grope toward reality by recalling every detail of the final illness.

An outsider cannot resolve the differences. We have no more hope of meeting conflicting needs than the grieving themselves. We can be sensitive, but we minister best by being present to the one person with whom we relate most easily and seeking other help for the rest.

We are dispensable. It is easy to love the vulnerable. We may grow very close and remain close for a lifetime. Or we may one day be left behind, lost in the pursuit of new interests and commitments that signal the end of grief. We must be ready to let go.

We have no answers

Throughout history, our race has struggled with the question of suffering. Many answers have been proposed, but none really satisfies until it is grasped at the far side of the question. Grieving people have to find their own answers in their own way. Until they do, the pat phrases well-meaning people hold out in consolation are words that only wound.

"You must be strong." For the children's sake, for the sake of the work that must be done, for their own sake—grieving people know the reasons they need strength. Needing it doesn't make it happen. Pointing out the need only accuses them of the failure they already feel. So do all the "musts": trust, believe, forgive, forget. It is hard enough to learn to do all those things without the burden of guilt for failure.

"You shouldn't feel that way." Feelings aren't rationally chosen. They are only felt. Augustine said it first: "Feelings are neither good nor bad." Moral choices lie in deciding what to do with the feelings—whether to set fire to the doctor's office or to allow him human fallibility.

"You'll marry again." Or have other children or keep the others already given. Somehow, the dead will be replaced—as though precious individuals were interchangeable, like spark plugs in an engine. There may indeed be others who will become as dear, but none of them can quite take the same place in a person's heart.

"You're doing so well." Standing straight and tall beside the casket, picking up the threads of life efficiently, tending to the financial settlement of the estate—many people have managed that in the initial numbness of loss. Then one day months after death, reality crashes in. They find themselves on a pedestal, admired by everyone for the illusion of strength that has sustained them so far. To whom can they confess that suddenly they are not doing well at all?

"It's for the best." Sometimes death is a kind end to suffering. But the investment of many hours of attention each day is a tender habit; sudden withdrawal hurts. Time hangs heavy, and the burden is sorely missed.

"It's God's will." Unarguable, perhaps, but hardly comforting. The faith that God's will is wholly loving, that he will bring good out of every evil is a faith not every believer possesses. Instead, the assurance of God's intent may create alienation, making a person feel like an insignificant puppet manipulated by a cruelly whimsical deity. God's will is life. God's will is the life-giving love we extend to one another.

11

Support for the Journey

If ministry to the bereaved asks us to be helpless, vulnerable, lacking in wisdom, why would anyone willingly accept such a state?

Because Jesus did. His passion and death is the only answer our God has ever given to the riddle of human pain. Jesus chose to *share* human failure as his path to triumphant glory. His resurrection is our pledge that meaning is offered on the other side of human sorrow.

And because, in our emptiness, we have much to receive from the sorrowing. They have entered the Lord's passion more deeply, more intimately than the rest of us. They can teach us sorrow's depth and breadth. They can give us deeper insight into what we mean when we say Jesus died for us. They can give us profound insight into the value of today's gifts of relationship.

To them we can only bring the gift of our helplessness. Walking together on grief's journey we come together to understanding, acceptance, affirmation and deeper faith.

Understanding

Understanding the grief process is not the same as understanding a person's grief. Nothing is the same as personal pain. It can be understood only by the one who feels it.

But knowing something of what people suffer in bereavement is the first step taken. It lets us hold a mirror up to them, to help them know that the frightening surge of emotion they feel is normal and finite. Just as mothers of toddlers find comfort in knowing all two-year-olds are stubborn and willful, grieving people hunger to know they have company in sorrow.

The key to helping someone to that certainty is *listening*—not just hearing what is said, but hearing the meaning behind the words and reflecting it.

Acceptance

Many feelings connected with grief are shameful. It is hard to speak of personal guilt. Nice people hide their anger—and believers are never angry at God. Sexuality is not laid in a partner's grave, but it seems wicked to hunger for touch, to yearn to feel sexually attractive.

Hidden feelings do not go away. Stifled emotion creates physical illness or explodes uncontrollably into psychological disorder. Feelings have to be owned before they can be healed.

Acceptance is the first step to ownership. If I can name my anger, my sexual hunger, I can begin to deal with it. But if you are shocked when I speak of it, I will bury it deeper and my problems are multiplied.

Affirmation

Another's acceptance of our darker feelings affirms that we are, in spite of our fears, lovable human beings. From infancy we all need that assurance.

Grieving people need it more than most. They are damaged; they are not the whole and capable persons they were before their loss. They need mirrors that are kind and reassuring. They need to know they look nice even though their eyes are red from crying; that they can still be loved and trusted though they let a loved one down. They need to believe that getting up and getting dressed this morning was indeed the triumph they think.

Shared faith

We minister in the name of Jesus Christ; why should we hesitate to speak his name? We don't have to be accomplished homilists— grieving people hear enough sermons anyway—to speak our sense of his nearness on the darkest day. If you pray for me, I'd like to know it. I'd wrap myself in the warmth of your prayers whenever the night is cold. And when God seems so far away, please carry me with you in your prayer. Take my hand and speak for me the words I cannot address to the Lord.

Sharing faith with the grieving just as often means sharing painful doubts and questions with no answers. Why do babies die? Does God take pleasure in seeing us suffer? Does he demand his pound of flesh before he will forgive our failings? Surely not, if the name we call him reflects anything of human fathering.

But confidence in our Father's tenderness lies far on the other side of the questions. People who have never questioned God are frightened at their own doubts. They think their agonizing questioning is a symptom of faith slipping away. More often, struggling with the questions leads to deeper faith. We can offer that assurance. Together we can talk to our Father, argue with him, yell at him sometimes, cry on his shoulder. And perhaps he will lead us— together—to deeper understanding.

Companionship

Grief is lonely. Because it threatens other, happier people, it isolates individuals. If someone listens and shares and sheds tears with another, it is still lonely. But not as much. "I do not believe," says Anne Morrow Lindbergh in *Hour of Gold, Hour of Lead*, "that sheer suffering teaches. If suffering alone taught, then all the world would be wise, since everyone suffers. To suffering must be added mourning, understanding, patience, love, openness and the willingness to remain vulnerable."

Establishing confidence

The widow whose husband's funeral you helped plan a month ago is unlikely to call you tomorrow and say, "I really feel awful; do you have time for a cup of coffee?" It takes time and repeated gestures of concern before your willingness to be there is that apparent, before another is really certain it is safe to trust you with the deepest, most painful feelings.

When death is new, whatever gesture you make is an invitation to trust. Before trust develops to a significant degree, you will have to call back again and again. Two to four weeks after the funeral, when the house has grown quiet and reality first begins to break through is an ideal time to begin.

Any excuse will do. Your community might decide, as mine did, to offer a book that views death and grief from a Christian perspective (see the bibliography, pp. 87-89). It is a way to say the grieving are still in the parish's thoughts and prayers. As grief develops, people try to articulate their feelings. A simple book helps them on their way.

Delaying to pick up dishes or chairs loaned at the time of the funeral is another tactic—though it may be undermined by scrupulous people.

The simplest approach is the most direct: to call or stop by "just because I was thinking about you." None of us, however independent we fancy ourselves, is adverse to being in another's loving thoughts.

"How are you doing?" is a ritual question; everyone knows the answer, "Fine." Repeated with genuine concern after a few minutes' conversation, it is no longer ritual. When I worked as a knitting instructor, a customer I had not seen for quite a while came in with a knitting problem. I answered her questions and then, sensing her tenseness, I asked her, "Tell me, how have you been?" To my horror she spent the next 15 minutes telling me about her son's suicide. But she came back often, with small knitting questions and a large need for someone who would simply listen to her.

To draw people out, address what you see. Is an outgoing person unusually quiet, or a gentle soul brusque and short? These are symptoms obvious as a rash. Name them. Ask if she is having a rough day or at whom he is angry. Your ability to name their feelings signals your willingness to accept them. Acceptance is really all you can offer, but if friends and relatives have tired of hearing about their sorrow, it may be a lot.

Speak your own feelings. We are not as different from one another as we like to think. If the death of your child is an event from which your imagination recoils, if you would be lonely without the spouse of a lifetime or angry with the partner who left you alone with those children, say so. You invite a response, even though it may be a contradiction: "No, I don't feel angry. I don't feel anything, just dead inside." Then you can talk about the other's feelings.

Talk about the dead. Many people won't; it seems a cruel reminder of the loss. But the loss is there, unavoidable, day in and day out. Memories are all that is left. Losing memories—or the right to speak them—only adds another loss. It seems as though no one else in the world believes the ended life was valuable enough to keep in the mind and heart. If you knew the deceased, share your memories. Drawn into ministry to a stranger, seek closer acquaintance with the person you have just missed.

For all our efforts, some will never unburden themselves. That is not a failure in our ministry. We are, after all, dealing with free persons, and the choice of a confidant is very personal. It is a gift of trust. Given, it is to be cherished; refused, even the refusal deserves respect.

Before feeling returns

Death is irreversible; the separation it creates will last a lifetime, not one day less. The struggle to grasp the fact needs sympathy and understanding—and support for the mechanisms that help bring the truth home.

Retelling the story of death is one such mechanism. The grieving may repeat the details of the final illness, the precise circumstances of the fatal accident beyond the tolerance of those who already know the story. It is not morbid fascination with death that prompts the telling. Memory haunts without mercy. The picture of a chubby toddler pops into the mind—replaced immediately by the picture of the same child lying pale and wasted in a hospital bed. The scene is replayed until its reality is integrated.

We may be the only ones still willing to listen, to allow someone to come to grips with the painful truth. Especially when shame is part of the picture—a drunken driver taking several lives, a son shot in the course of a robbery—listening affirms the dead were persons worth mourning, whatever their failings.

The presence of the dead is often felt as keenly as their absence. A widow whose husband collapsed and died wordlessly dreams he returns to speak a tender goodbye. A widower hears his wife call his name so clearly he turns to answer. Her perfume hangs in the air, but she is not there. A word of comfort from the other side of the grave or an attempt by the subconscious mind to recover the loss? No one knows for sure. But people who see things that are not there wonder if they are losing their minds. Hallucination is a symptom of a disturbed mind, except in grief. There, it is a common experience, and we can offer that reassurance.

Dealing with denial

Numbness consciously sustained is more difficult to handle. Sometimes it requires professional help we are not qualified to give.

The search for numbness may not be consciously deliberate, and often it isn't. We can ask the questions to bring it to conscious attention. "Does working (or playing) so hard help you forget your grief?" "Do you think you will leave your memories behind if you move?" No one abandons a scheme that might work; only a fool would try to talk someone out of it. The fortunate discover the plan's futility without burning their bridges behind them.

When my father died, my mother talked about moving back to the town where they had lived most of their married life. None of us could understand; the climate and activities in their retirement home obviously suited her very well. After she spent a summer in our home town, she explained it for us. "I couldn't find him there," she admitted, and decided to stay where she was in peace. We cannot, of course, make these decisions for others. But we can encourage them to leave their options open.

More dangerous escapes beckon the bereaved. Sleeping pills, tranquilizers, alcohol offer to prolong the numbness and hold the pain at bay. They are readily available, often urged on people in the weeks after death by well-meaning friends.

There is a fine line between emotional dependency and chemical dependency. Once a person has stepped over the line, he or she needs more helping skills than we have to offer. We can mirror their need and encourage them to seek qualified help as soon as they can admit their need.

Easing anger

Nice people don't harbor anger. We know that; as Christians we have heard about forgiveness. When loss leaves anger in its wake, good people are ashamed of their feelings. But grieving people are more passive than active; they do not so much harbor anger as find themselves helpless in its grip.

We talk about Jesus' anger in the temple; we say anger is justified when circumstances trample innocent people underfoot. Grieving people have a right to be angry. Death has taken control over their lives and they are trampled.

Anger has physical effects. Adrenalin surges through the body. Muscles tighten, teeth clench, the body makes ready for combat. Without a release, the body wages war on itself. At best, a tension headache ruins the day. In time, more serious disorders may arise. Some outlet must be found for that physical tension.

Just talking about it helps. A high school counselor I know tells how a very angry father stormed into her office one day. For 10 minutes, he expressed his dislike of everything about the school in certain terms and high volume. She listened patiently, making no comment and offering no defense. At last he sighed, leaned back into his chair, visibly relaxing as he asked, "What do you think we should do about it?" Her acceptance of his anger allowed him to release it harmlessly and move on. Our acceptance is no less healing for the grieving who make us the targets of pent-up feelings.

Physical activity is another outlet. Throwing a tennis ball against the basement wall or a rolled-up sock in the living room is something we can suggest. Dr. Elisabeth Kubler-Ross gives dying patients and their families a length of rubber hose with which to attack a pillow. The suggestion affirms the justice and acceptability of their anger.

Kubler-Ross warns us God is often the target of human anger. But he, she reminds, can take it. We often offer "God's will" as a reason to comfort the sorrowing without realizing it is, in the same breath, blame. God is our loving Father; surely he knows his children are prone to tantrums. He made us and knows our need to vent our anger. If we let him, he will hold us tightly so we cannot hurt ourselves until the storm has passed.

If other believers are shocked at a mourner's anger, that person will not reveal it again. They will try to hide it even from themselves and from God. But if anger is all they have to speak to God, best they speak it. Otherwise they have nothing to say to him and will grow silently distant. The only way to resolve a quarrel with another person is to talk it over—even when the other person is God.

Relieving guilt

Death—especially sudden death or suicide—casts a glaring light on the most ordinary human failure. Columnist Mike Royko, writing after his wife's death, sought to relieve others of the burden he carried. "Do her and me a favor," he wrote. "If there's someone you love but haven't said so in a while, say it now. Always, always, say it now."

It's good advice; we'd all be happier if we followed it. We don't. And when death has robbed people of the chance, they seldom deny their guilt. They torture themselves with it.

Human guilt can be forgiven. God does it every day. Sacramental reconciliation is one way to feel his forgiving touch. Another is to read the gospels: Jesus was never harsh with those who acknowledged their failures. He condemned only the self-righteous.

Where guilt cannot be seen but for the clear vision of retrospect,

forgiveness is harder to accept. Most of us would have acted
differently 10 years ago had we known then what we know today.
Could we see a clot forming in a narrowed artery, or a truck bearing
down on our car, we would cherish every moment of today and
lavish attention on the people we love.

Mostly we stumble along, careless with the relationships we hold
most dear. Mostly we do the best we can in the midst of life's
pressures. And if tomorrow disaster strikes, we will need to hear
others say, over and over again, that we did do the best we could in
light of what we knew, with no time to think about it.

No death leaves a greater burden of guilt than a suicide. The
failure to hold a loved one in life—even to notice the signs of despair
—cuts deeply. Too deeply sometimes for acknowledgment. Many
people will refuse to speak the truth about the death, even to
themselves. Death becomes an accident. He didn't realize the garage
door was closed; she didn't know the gun was loaded; a sudden dizzy
spell prevented a person from moving out of harm's way.

Real failure or guilt cannot be healed by denial. Only forgiveness
heals guilt. False guilt must be carried as long as the lie lives. Very
gently, the suicides' families must be led to admit the truth.

Lightening depression

Depression is described as an excessive weight carried day in and
day out. It saps energy, erodes sleep, explodes over minor irritations.
People find it difficult to move out of depression alone.

A long period of depression calls for more active intervention on
our part than any of grief's other emotions. We cannot brighten the
darkness but we can make ourselves available to sit in it with
another. Like children, we are more at ease in the dark when we
have company.

It's a good time to extend an invitation for lunch, for a shopping
trip, simply to share a cup of coffee. Timidly phrased, the invitation
is likely to be refused. Reaching out to grasp a hand requires an
effort beyond the capabilities of the truly depressed. Be almost
mandatory: "Come and have a cup of tea with me." "I'll pick you up
at 1:00."

Spontaneous invitations seem the most compelling. Two of the
dearest friends I have made responded first to words I spoke without
thinking at the end of a weekday morning mass: a young widow who

came home with me for a cup of coffee and an elderly widow who accepted a ride home and has been riding with me ever since.

The unexpected gift of practical help resurrects hope. The needs so acute the day of the funeral no longer exist by the time depression sets in. By then, people have learned to manage household tasks and family support all alone. But the gift of an hour free from responsibility can lift a heavy burden. It's all right, the gesture says, to find the day's demands overwhelming. But you don't have to do it all alone.

In depression, the sense of self-worth sinks with the spirits. If she were competent, she wouldn't have such a hard time managing alone. If he were loving, he could meet the children's need for attention. We all need verbal strokes from time to time; grieving people need them more. Be specific in your compliments, but be careful about painting glowing pictures. Don't praise a heroism the sorrowing person may not feel he or she possesses. Praise the way a person looks, a specific thing they have accomplished.

Borrow on their gifts. We know we take as much as we give, but grieving people find that hard to believe. Request advice or ask to learn a skill or copy a recipe. Show the sorrowing their gifts, their worth.

Tears and touch

In the frantic rediscovery of sexual pleasure, our society seems to have forgotten the simpler human need to express emotion. Touch is taboo, even among members of the same sex, and tears are threatening.

Grieving people cry—even men. Tears are a hard lump in the back of the throat or an acid drip into the stomach, but they are there. The best place for them is on the cheeks. There is a vast difference between making someone cry and allowing them to weep—even helping them shed their tears.

Cruelty makes people cry and death is cruel. But people who share the loss and feel another's pain are not cruel. They are helpful.

When the tears have fallen what do you do? If you find moisture welling in your eyes, that's all right. Sympathetic people sometimes cry, too. I wish I could cry that easily. I don't but there is another response I make. Tears are the first language any human being uses to express pain. And everyone knows what to do with a crying baby: Pick him up and hold him tight.

Adults who weep need to be held, too. If circumstances or the limits of your personality exclude a warm embrace (I would hesitate to hug some widowers), a pat on the shoulder or taking of the hand expresses the same warm comfort.

Jesus wept, so those who cry are in the best of company. It's all right to cry in the presence of death's loss.

Acknowledging inadequacy

Caring and presence are not always enough, even when done in the name of Jesus Christ. We can support people in normal grief. But not all grief falls within the normal limits. When signs indicate abnormal grief, we must seek more competent help.

When grief's ordinary symptoms are extreme, danger is brewing. Failure to show signs of grief is a warning signal in a person of ordinary (not stoic) reserve and composure. Hysteria in a normally stable personality, extreme hostility, gradual and continual withdrawal from usual interests, the development of a major illness or a host of minor physical symptoms may indicate great emotional disturbance.

Where several symptoms coexist, the warning is clear. That person needs more help than we can give. We must extend to ourselves the same acceptance of inadequacy we give the grieving. It's all right to be short of skills. If we really were self-sufficient, there would be no need for a Christian community.

12

Broadly Based Support

Support for the grieving is not our exclusive function. The task does not belong to us alone; the whole community is called to serve the sorrowing. Helping others exercise their baptismal commitment is an important element of our ministry.

Friends and neighbors withdraw from the grieving, not because they don't care, but because they don't understand the inner conflict, because they don't know what to say or do. They need assurance that another's grief is normal and that the greatest help they can give is acceptance. They need to learn how to share their gifts.

One young widow left with two children and a business to run coped bravely with all the demands she faced. Her day's weakest point was the dinner hour. Tired from work, she found it hard to cook. Night after night she yielded to her children's request for hamburgers. Finally, six months after her husband's death, she confessed that the very thought of the great American delicacy sickened her.

Her neighbors were kind and caring people, deeply concerned for her. But they hesitated to call. They knew how hard she was working; they feared any show of concern would disrupt her busy day. When I told one neighbor about the hamburger habit, the whole street was quick to respond. Glad to know how to help, they brought casseroles and dropped casual dinner invitations. The widow speaks of them with warmth. "I never could have made it without them," she says.

There are many small ways in which neighbors and friends can become involved with the needs of the grieving. And when neighbors are worn out by caring for several stricken families or short on particular skills, the resources of the community at large can always be summoned.

Support groups

No one knows better than someone who's been there: that's the rationale for support groups. In a large group, each person's grief can find an echo in another's experience.

One mother I know had buried a daughter after a long battle with cancer. She was very defensive about the uniqueness of *her* sorrow. Another mother's dead child was only an infant; her daughter stood on the threshold of maturity. Another young woman died swiftly and suddenly; that mother was spared the agony of watching slow decline.

In an organization of bereaved parents, she could at last find understanding. There she found other parents who had lost to cruel disease a child on the verge of adulthood. They understood how she felt. They could challenge her to move through her grief, because they had lived with their own a little longer.

Common experience can be narrowed as far as numbers permit: widows, widowers, people now alone after a lifetime of marriage, people with young children to raise. Their needs are similar but at the same time different. In my city, there are different groups for bereaved parents: mothers, fathers, parents whose children were murdered, crib deaths, cancer victims. Grieving parents whose need is very great sometimes attend several of them.

The crucial element in a support group is the presence of real survivors—people who have worked through their grief or who are at least farther down the road than the newcomers. Without that element the group will only share pain without hope.

Support groups are easy to form. (Even strangers at a cocktail party share experiences with each other.) Grieving people know what they have in common. Bringing them together as often as possible is one way the community can express its care. In Catholic communities, an occasional memorial mass and reception is a natural focus.

The decision to meet more often belongs to the grieving themselves. We can suggest it, but they must choose how often to meet and what to do. Some groups may simply want an opportunity to talk to others who understand. Others will prefer a more formal structure with outside speakers to help them deal, for instance, with grief in their children. Still others may look for more social activities.

People new to grief have little interest in support groups. They might learn of a group's existence, but real interest develops only as they begin to struggle with their feelings and to wonder if they are really normal. As their need for reassurance develops and they begin to ask about others' feelings and circumstances, we can say more about the groups available. Whenever possible, let someone from the group make contact. No one else can explain so well what the organization offers to an individual.

Even where no group is available, putting people in touch with each other makes mutual gifts available. When our second daughter was born 20 years ago, very premature and very sick, I received a note from a neighbor whose baby had survived a similar brush with death. I read it over and over, clinging to the understanding she offered. I still remember how much comfort she gave.

Who ministers to the ministers?

Being fully present to the sorrowing is draining. It hurts. It empties you until there seems to be nothing left to give.

I was very personally involved in the funeral of a young woman I had seen grow from awkward girlhood to graceful maturity and come to love as a friend along the way. Her parents too were friends, my neighbors across the street. After her death, I ran back and forth across the street with my poor gifts of food, I made phone calls, I shared their tears and helped to organize the neighbors' support. By the morning of the funeral, I was empty. I was to read that afternoon, to offer the comfort of God's word to those people, and I didn't know how I was going to do it.

In desperation, I called a close friend, a priest. "Have you ever felt like this?" I asked. "What do you do?"

His response was gentle. "Carol, you of all people must know what I do. I call my friends." In a flash I remembered his phone calls, his stories of tragedies, his requests for prayers. Putting my concerns in his caring hands gave me what I needed to go on. I have never forgotten his advice.

People who share others' pain need one another. We need to meet frequently to trade stories, to ask advice, to reassure one another that the little we give is enriched by the Lord's power. And we need to pray together.

That was the first lesson we learned when we formed our parish bereavement ministry. We can't do anything without the Lord's help. Once a month we meet for an hour of sharing and prayer. We listen to the message of scripture. We pray for the families entrusted to our care. We pray for one another. We share the joys and the pain of our ministry, and sometimes laugh that the Lord should be so careless in his choice of instruments.

What we give to the grieving among us, I cannot really measure, for I have never lost someone from the very center of my life. What we give to one another, I know and treasure. Love and faith are not gifts we are given to keep, but something we borrow wherever we find them.

In the people with whom I share this ministry I have seen more love and sensitivity than I dared to dream exists in this sinful world. From them, and from the people who have so generously shared their sorrow with me, I have learned that the Lord is very near to his people.

For you and for your community, I wish no less.

Bibliography

Experience is the best teacher, but we are wise to undergird experience with the wisdom of those who have preceded us. A good library of books and tapes is invaluable for a bereavement ministry—and sometimes offers the support a grieving person needs and cannot find at home. The following list is far from complete, but it is a good beginning.

The death experience

On Death and Dying, by Elisabeth Kubler-Ross. This landmark study of dying patients created an interest in death and grief. Although concerned with the loss felt by the dying, the principles given apply also to grief—or any other loss. MacMillan Publishing Company (New York, 1969). Paperback, 289 pp.

Concerning Death: A Practical Guide for the Living, by Earl A. Grollman. A comprehensive treatment of death from many vantage points: religious perspectives, funeral practices, practical concerns, grief. Beacon Press (Boston, 1974). Paperback, 365 pp.

Understanding grief

A Time to Grieve, by Ken Czillinger. In words culled from the grieving people to whom he has ministered, a priest explores the elements of grief and healing. NCR Cassettes (Kansas City, 1980). 8 cassettes.

A Grief Observed, by C.S. Lewis. A journal kept by a talented writer during the months after his wife's death. Bantam Books (New York, 1961). Paperback, 151 pp.

Learning to Live Again: The Journey Through Grief for the Widowed and

Divorced, by Judith Tate. Four people tell their personal stories of loss and healing against a commentary on the grief process. St. Anthony Messenger Press (Cincinnati, 1979). Paperback, 184 pp.

The Widower, by Jane Burgess Kohn and Willard K. Kohn. The particular needs of widowed men. Beacon Press (Boston, 1978). Hardcover, 166 pp.

The Bereaved Parent, by Harriet Sarnoff Schiff. From her own experience and that of others who have lost a child, a bereaved mother offers hope to stricken parents and a wealth of insight to the rest of us. Penguin Books (New York, 1978). Paperback, 146 pp.

Telling a Child About Death, by Edgar N. Jackson. The central questions and external expressions of children's grief. Hawthorne Books (New York, 1965). Paperback, 91 pp.

Talking About Death: A Dialogue Between Parent and Child, by Earl A. Grollman. Sample dialogue to read or carry on with a child, with an explanation of the underlying reasons. Beacon Press (Boston, 1976). Paperback, 98 pp.

Together by Your Side, by Rev. Joseph M. Champlin. A taped training course in ministry to the sick, the dying and the bereaved. Includes leader's guide and other resources. Ave Maria Press (Notre Dame, 1980), 3 cassettes.

May I Hate God? by Pierre Wolff. Deals not only with the questions of anger and guilt but also with the helping response. Includes Scripture texts for prayer during anger. Paulist Press (New York, 1979). Paperback, 76 pp.

When Bad Things Happen to Good People, by Harold S. Kushner. A rabbi, himself a bereaved father, explores the reasons for human suffering. Solid biblical basis and emphasis on community make the theology readily accessible to Christians. Avon (New York, 1981). Paperback, 149 pp.

Gift books for the grieving

Beyond Sorrow: Reflections on Death and Grief, by Herb and Mary Montgomery. Attractively illustrated reflections on the questions and emotions that follow death. Winston Press (Minneapolis, 1977). Paperback, 62 pp.

Be Comforted, by Rev. Joseph T. Nolan. A brief meditation on death from the Christian perspective; color photographs. Franciscan Communications Center (Los Angeles, 1978). Paperback, 12 pp.

For liturgy planners

The Rite of Funerals, translated by the International Commission on English in the Liturgy. Of particular importance is the introduction, which explains the rite's principles.

Loving and Dying: A Commentary on the Lectionary Texts for Weddings and Funerals, by Donald Senior, C.P. Especially helpful is the list of themes and related passages on p. 39. Celebration Books (Kansas City, 1979). Paperback, 88 pp. (52 on funeral readings).

Music in Catholic Worship. Basic principles. United States Catholic Conference (Washington, D.C., 1972). Paperback, 22 pp.

Guidelines for Effective Worship, by Eugene A. Walsh, S.S. A simple presentation of the structure of the Mass, distinguishing between principal and secondary elements. North American Liturgy Resources (Phoenix, 1974). Paperback, 14 pp.

Through Death to Life, by Rev. Joseph M. Champlin. An inexpensive collection of the funeral texts, easy to carry and share. Ave Maria Press (Notre Dame, 1979). Paperback, 87 pp.

Human resources

The Society of Compassionate Friends, an organization for bereaved parents with many local chapters. National headquarters: P.O. Box 1347, Oakbrook, IL 60521.

NAIM Conference, an organization of Catholic widowers and widows. National headquarters: 109 N. Dearborn St., Chicago, IL 60602.

Parents Without Partners, an interfaith organization for parents left by death or divorce to raise children alone. National headquarters: 7910 Woodmont Ave., Washington, DC 20014.

THEOS (They Help Each Other Spiritually), a nondenominational, spiritually oriented support group for young and middle-aged widowed people with children. National headquarters: 10521 Lindberg Ave., Pittsburgh, PA 15235.

The Beginning Experience offers a weekend to help the widowed and divorced work through their grief. National headquarters: 4503 Bridge St., Fort Worth, TX 76103.

In addition, many organizations supporting research into a particular disease offer support to the victim's family. Two notable examples are the

American Cancer Society, 219 East 42nd St., New York, NY 10017, and the National Foundation for Sudden Infant Death, 1501 Broadway, New York, NY 10036.